'In this refreshing, ~~rigorous~~ ████ ███book, Christopher Ash strips marriage down to ████████uals. Engaged couples enmeshed in wedding planning ar. ███arried couples set up for disappointment by Hollywood-style thinking need to read it. The book acts as a corrective to exaggerated claims and self-indulgent attitudes concerning marriage endemic in our culture, and becomes a call to joyful biblical simplicity and true God-centred liberty in marriage.'
John Benton (Pastor, Chertsey Street Baptist Church, Guildford and Editor, Evangelicals Now*) and Ann Benton (Chairman, London Women's Convention)*

'Married for God provides an invaluable challenge to deepen and strengthen relationships, through a fresh understanding of God's purpose for marriage. A passionate and discerning reminder that getting the best out of marriage is not achieved by focusing on what we want from it, but on what God wants to accomplish through it.'
Jason Gardner (LICC Youth Project Researcher) and Rachel Gardner (Creative Director, The Romance Academy)

'Christopher Ash's book is firmly biblical and exegetical, but at the same time well related to the realities of modern life and contemporary issues with all their pressures on marriage relationships. Some will question his exegesis on submission and obedience, but will be challenged and cheered by his emphasis that marriage is not just for the selfish pleasure of the couple concerned. It is particularly for the glory of God and for the service of the church and world in which God has placed us. So this book is definitely different from the mass of other books on marriage and I would warmly commend it. I shall recommend it to people starting out on the adventure of marriage and to others who may have been married for some years. An excellent, challenging and helpful book.'
Martin and Elizabeth Goldsmith, Conference Speakers, and Associate Lecturers, All Nations Christian College

To Alex and katrina

Married
for God

With love from

Table 5 Alive!

Christopher Ash

Married for God

Making your marriage the best it can be

ivp

INTER-VARSITY PRESS
Norton Street, Nottingham NG7 3HR, England
Email: ivp@ivpbooks.com
Website: www.ivpbooks.com

First published 2007
Reprinted 2007, 2008, 2009, 2011, 2012

British Library Cataloguing in Publication Data
A catalogue record for this book is available from the British Library.

ISBN 978–1–84474–189–2

Set in 11.5/14pt Dante
Typeset in Great Britain by CRB Associates, Potterhanworth, Lincolnshire
Printed and bound in Great Britain by Ashford Colour Press Ltd, Gosport,
Hampshire

*Inter-Varsity Press publishes Christian books that are true to the Bible and that
communicate the gospel, develop discipleship and strengthen the church for its
mission in the world.*

*Inter-Varsity Press is closely linked with the Universities and Colleges Christian
Fellowship, a student movement connecting Christian Unions in universities and
colleges throughout Great Britain, and a member movement of the International
Fellowship of Evangelical Students. Website: www.uccf.org.uk*

Contents

Acknowledgments

I want to say a special thank-you to those who read and commented on the manuscript, including Stuart Allen, Carolyn Bickersteth, Andy Bleach, Sandra Byatt, Mary Davis, Andrew Leonard, Steve Midgley, Mark O'Donoghue, and Phil and Christine Mulryne. I am of course responsible for the final version, but it is all the better for their help and advice. My warm thanks are also due to all my colleagues at the Proclamation Trust for their encouragement. And I am grateful to my editor, Eleanor Trotter at IVP, for her wise advice and steady encouragement.

Above all I want to thank my dear wife Carolyn for showing me so much of the joy and purpose of marriage in practice as well as in theory. Thank you for your patience with an imperfect husband who pontificates about marriage while he ought to be getting on and living it.

Preface

Is this book for you?

Sex shouts at us in every movie, from every bus and poster, and from every shelf of the station bookstall. Well, not every one; but enough to make a strong impression on us. The combination of this pressure with our own natural desires is explosive. My guess is that Christians who say they never struggle in this area are dishonest on this point. We need help. This book is a straightforward account of what the Bible teaches about marriage.

If you are engaged, I hope this book will help you prepare for marriage. I hope you will find here Bible teaching to consider together as a couple that will shape your hopes and expectations in a really healthy way.

If you are in the first few years of marriage (or even later), I hope this book will help you lay foundations for a good marriage. Whether you received good marriage preparation or none, I hope this presentation of the Bible's teaching will challenge and refresh you both.

If you are single and wondering whether to get married, I hope this book is for you. I hope you will find here clear Bible teaching about what marriage is, and – more important – what is the point and purpose of marriage.

If you are single and disappointed, because the opportunity for marriage has not (yet) come your way, I hope that you too will find here some comfort and encouragement to live your present unmarried life wholeheartedly and joyfully for Christ.

And, for that matter, if you have no intention of being married, this book may help you understand and encourage those who are.

There are questions for private study and/or group discussion at the end of each chapter. A selection of these could form the basis of a Marriage Preparation Course or a Marriage Refresher Course, for couples on their own or for a larger group.

Christopher Ash
London
March 2007

Introduction: God at the centre

In the beginning, God...
(Genesis 1:1)

Jane and Dave were on the way to their first marriage
preparation course meeting. They had recently got engaged
and the minister had asked to see them. Neither admitted it
to the other, but they were pretty nervous.

To break the tension Dave asked Jane, 'What are you
hoping to get out of these meetings?' and it led to a useful
discussion. They agreed that they wanted help with good
communication, so that Dave would learn to communicate
(rare, in a man, as Jane said) and that Jane could
communicate a bit less mysteriously ('So that I can
understand what you really mean,' as Dave put it). They
looked forward to hearing how to relate to both sets of
parents (not always the easiest people, they both agreed).
They were beginning to think through the issue of handling
money, and thought they might pick up some useful wisdom
on that score. They were a bit shy about admitting it, but

each hoped secretly that they might pick up tips on helping *sex* to go well. And, having just had a painful disagreement (why does this have to happen just before marriage preparation?), they wondered if the meeting with the minister might help with patching up and moving on.

So they were a bit disappointed when the minister said they ought to begin by talking about God...

The Bible begins with God. From page one, God is at the centre. I want that to be true of this book. I make no apology for that.

What do you expect in a marriage book? John Gray's best-seller *Men are from Mars, Women are from Venus* is subtitled *A practical guide to getting what you want in your relationships.* Maybe that is what you expect: a guide to getting what *you* want.

You will find this sort of guide not only in secular bookshops but also on church bookstalls. One Christian book was subtitled *Achieve a happy and more fulfilling relationship.* A Christian marriage course offered 'a blueprint for happiness with your partner'.

This book won't help you with that sort of thing, because it is about God more than it is about you and me. In some ways it would be easier to write a book of common-sense wisdom and practical advice about sex and marriage, glossing it with a Christian veneer. Instead, I want to start, continue and finish the book with God firmly at the centre. He is our Maker and he will be our Judge. We need to listen to him.

What is the point of marriage? Or, to be more basic, what is the point of sex? We in the West are obsessed with sex. It used to be said that the Victorians were embarrassed about sex but obsessed with death. For us it is the opposite: we are embarrassed about death but obsessed with sex. And yet relationships are breaking down all around us. 'People change their marriage partner faster than they change our brand of washing machine,' claims an advertiser. A newspaper reports on an American entrepreneur who offers wedding rings for hire to save wasting money on buying one for a marriage that may not last long. Outside marriage, relationships break down even faster; indeed, a lot faster. We live in a world marked by what has been called 'the churning of partners'.

We are bound to be worried by this. If you are thinking of getting married, at the back of your mind this anxiety will lurk. If you are married, you will be unsettled every time a friend's marriage breaks down. Somehow the draught of someone else's breakdown seems to blow through – and threaten – our own marriages.

Why do relationships break down? There are all sorts of reasons. But one of the biggest is disappointment. We wouldn't start unless we had hopes, whether or not we spell them out. When our goals are frustrated, we are tempted to cut and run. So I want to begin with the question *'What ought our purpose to be?'* What are proper hopes and aims for marriage?

Some marriage books focus on the 'How?' questions. How can we communicate better? How can we have better sex? How can we resolve conflict? And so on. These questions have their place, but for the most part I am not going to focus on them.

Other books (more theoretical ones) focus on the 'What?' questions, issues of definition. What is marriage? Does it have boundaries? Is living together the same as marriage? And so on. These too are important questions, but again I am not going to major on them.

It is good to start with the 'Why?' questions. If we get our aims clear, then we shall see *why* marriage has to be *what* it is, and we will be well placed to see *how* to build a strong marriage.

I want to begin with a fundamental statement:

■ **We ought to want what God wants in marriage.**

Or, to put it another way, God's 'Why?' matters more than my 'Why?' To put God at the centre like this will turn our thinking upside down. Sometimes in churches we get the impression that God exists to help me do better in life. I come to God because he can help me with my marriage. He is my lifestyle coach, and with a bit of luck and a favourable wind, and if I 'pay' him enough with prayer and a bit of well-chosen religious activity, then he will line up his energies behind my goals. He will help me achieve what I want. In marriage he will help me to be happy and satisfied.

The truth is the exact opposite. You and I need to ask God what he wants and then line up our goals behind his, rather than expecting him to line up his goals behind ours. There are at least two reasons for this.

The first has to do with right and wrong. God has given us all we have. Every good and perfect gift comes from him (James 1:17); therefore the most basic thing human beings ought to do is to honour him and give thanks (Romans 1:21) and to love him with all our hearts and minds (Matthew 22:37–38). As a matter of simple morality we ought to ask what he wants and not expect him to want what we want. And this includes sex.

The second reason is practical: what he wants is (by definition) in line with how the world actually is and how we are made. Because he is the Creator, living in line with his purposes is for our best. This is very hard for us to grasp. For example, the writer Will Self puts it well when he says that in our culture right and wrong are not part of 'the very structure of the universe' but 'a matter of personal taste akin to a designer label, sewn into the inside lining of conscience'. You choose your own right and wrong; it is a personal lifestyle choice. Against this, the Christian holds that right and wrong are to the universe what an animal's skin is to an animal. Just as an animal cannot change its coat, so we cannot choose our personal 'right and wrong' as we might pick a coat from the wardrobe. God has made the world with structure and order, not just physical order (which science explores) but moral order. This is the Bible concept of 'wisdom', which is the blueprint or architecture according to which the world is built: 'The LORD by wisdom founded the earth' (Proverbs 3:19).

So, when we ask what God wants, we are asking what is best for us. What is best for us is not what we want, but what he wants. When I ask what God wants for marriage, I am saying that I want my marriage to cut with the grain of the universe.

So I need to begin our study with a call to repentance. That sounds old-fashioned. But it is just what we need: to change our minds, consciously to turn from what we want – from our hopes for marriage – and to seek his will and goals for marriage. If you are a couple preparing for marriage, will you line up your goals with God's purposes? If you are married, will you realign your hopes with what God wants? Will you want what God wants for your marriage? If you are unmarried, will you too resolve to serve God wholeheartedly with the opportunities that your singleness offers?

But what does God want for marriage? Why did God choose to create humankind male and female? Presumably he did not need to do it this way. A friend of mine used to point out that God could have made all human beings like an amoeba which, when it wants to multiply, simply divides. But he chose to make us men and women, with all the wonderful and mysterious chemistry of sexual desire and delight. Why did he do this? What is his aim? Most of this book explores the answer to that question. You will find here not lifestyle tips but a serious engagement with Christian belief about God. And yet, surprisingly, you will make a better marriage if you focus on God and not on marriage. Put God at the centre, and strive to want what he wants.

For study or discussion

1. Why is it important to ask about the 'why' of marriage before we tackle the 'what' and the 'how'?

2. For what reasons ought we to put God at the centre?

3. Take time out for some quiet prayer at the start of these studies. Consciously and deliberately ask God to help you put him and his purposes at the centre.

1 A word about baggage and grace

Ann felt numb inside. She had put her trust in Jesus Christ just six months earlier. Tonight she was going on her first date with a Christian man. Mike seemed to have had such a straightforward past – a loving Christian home, a real Christian faith for as long as he could remember, and no serious girlfriend ever before. And now he had asked her, Ann, out.

She found him very attractive, both physically and as a Christian friend she respected and whose company she loved. She ought to have felt excited. And yet she felt numb. Because her past was such a mess by comparison. And now it all came flooding back: the dysfunctional home with her parents' messy divorce and her two very temporary 'stepfathers'; the awful peer pressure at school not to be a 'virgin' (despicable term of abuse, how she dreaded that word); the night she was pressurized into sleeping with a boy for the first time; the gradual descent into cheap sex that made her feel dirty but that she yet could not resist for fear of not being loved.

> By now she was almost hard-wired to expect a date to end with bed. She knew in her head it had to be different. But she was paralysed with fear and regret. 'How can *I* be a Christian?' she asked herself. 'I am dirty; spoiled goods. Purity is a dream for others, but can never be true for me.' And yet she longed for purity.
>
> And so when Mike arrived at the door, instead of the happy relaxed Ann he had known in the church twenties group, he met a tense girl with traces of tears on her cheeks.

As we embark on our study of the Bible, I want to devote the first chapter to the subject of grace. This is very important. Unless we understand grace, we will misunderstand all the Bible's teaching about sex and marriage. It is grace that Ann needs, and actually it is grace that Mike needs, just as much. Unless we begin with grace we shall end with either despair or self-righteousness.

I hope that this book will do more than give information. I want us all to be changed by God as we engage with the Bible's teaching about sex and marriage. This is meant to be a book that persuades as well as informs. But I need to be realistic, because both you and I bring to sex and marriage all sorts of baggage. We bring baggage personally from our individual stories. And we bring baggage corporately from the culture to which we belong. We do not 'walk' into this book, or into marriage for that matter, as free individuals travelling light. We stagger in, burdened by all sorts of suitcases full of our histories and our culture. That is as true for Mike as it is for Ann; as true for me as it is for you.

Personally, we have our own histories of sexual experience or inexperience; of hopes realized or deferred; of longings or aversions; of fulfilment or frustration; of fears, anxieties, delights, regrets. What we have done or not done, how we have been treated or mistreated by others: all these things shape what we believe.

Some of us want to justify our behaviour. So we want a belief system that plays us onside by saying that what we have done was OK. We want to be able to say, 'It was understandable – even right and good – that I did this or that. I can be proud, or at least not ashamed, that I behaved like that.'

Or, if we know our behaviour was wrong, we may be paralysed, as Ann was, by regrets and a feeling that we have 'mucked up' and can't make a fresh start. Or maybe you have been abused or pressured into sexual behaviour of which you are ashamed, even though it may not have been your fault. All of this deeply affects the way we come to this subject.

Corporately, we all belong to a culture that suggests that sex is OK in all sorts of relationships. Every soap opera, every movie, every magazine article portrays as normal these easy behaviours and attitudes towards sex. They invite us to belong to the culture by sharing those attitudes. We are shaped by our surroundings much more than we like to admit.

Because sexual feelings affect us so deeply, we need to be realistic about our fragility and the baggage and damage we bring to the subject. You and I do not listen neutrally to the Bible's teaching, waiting like a clean sheet of paper for God to write his will onto us. Our sheets of paper are already covered with scribbles, crossings out, and more scribbles. We come as bundles of prejudices with our ears at best half open.

So before I invite you to come with me to be transformed by the Bible's teaching, I want to say three basic things about God and sex. All three are to do with grace.

The Bible speaks to those whose sexual pasts are spoiled

[9]Do you not know that the unrighteous will not inherit the kingdom of God? Do not be deceived: neither the sexually immoral, nor idolaters, nor adulterers, nor men who practise homosexuality, [10]nor thieves, nor the greedy, nor drunkards,

nor revilers, nor swindlers will inherit the kingdom of God.
[11]And such were some of you. But you were washed, you were
sanctified, you were justified in the name of the Lord Jesus
Christ and by the Spirit of our God.
(1 Corinthians 6:9–11)

The first truth is this: the Bible speaks to men and women who
are all spoiled in the area of sex. We tend to think Christianity
is for those who are sexual successes, those who have got it
together, those who are respectable, or those who have clean
histories. Quite the opposite is true. Writing to the young
Christians in Corinth, Paul gives a terrible list of wrongdoing,
including sexual mess-ups. And then he says, 'And such were
some of you.' If the stories of the men and women in the Corinth
church were told, some of them would not be suitable for
children to hear. They would include the most terrible stories of
moral messes in the area of sex. I doubt if any story told to a
minister or doctor today about sexual confusion and mess would
be worse than the stories Paul must have heard in Corinth. They
would have included casual sex, abuse (from both victims and
perpetrators), homosexual practice, and probably much more.

There is an old joke in which a man asks a passer-by the way
to somewhere. When the passer-by learns where this person
wants to go, he replies, 'Well, if I were you, I wouldn't start
from here.' Some people think Christianity is like that: when
we ask about the right way to live, Christianity says, 'Well, if I
were you, I wouldn't start from where *you* are. You have blown
it already; there is no hope for you.' Again, the opposite is the
case. Jesus the great doctor came for the sick, not for those who
thought they were well (Matthew 9:12–13). This book is not for
the Pharisee who thanks God that he has a clear record in sex,
unlike those rotten people he reads about in the tabloids. It is
for the failure who says: 'God, be merciful to me, a sinner!'
(Luke 18:9–14).

This truth cuts two ways. If I think I am basically pretty

much in the clear (as perhaps Mike thought), it teaches me that I am not, and reminds me that in the area of my sexual desires, even if not my actions, I fall far short of purity of heart. But on the other hand, if, like Ann, I am very conscious of my failures and carry the scars around with me, it says to me that Jesus Christ came precisely for me.

Reading this book, you may think that I, the writer, have got it together and won the moral battles in the area of sex. You may think that because I have a lovely wife and four children, it's all right for me. How wrong you would be. I have been given a very lovely wife, and I thank God for her; but there are times when she and I struggle to relate in love, when we quarrel, when things are cold and painful between us. We have been entrusted with three sons and a daughter, and we thank God for them. But there are times when being parents is pretty tough for us and full of pain, as it is for most parents. And I'm sure that there are times for them when being our children is pretty tough for them too! Twenty-five years after getting married my sexual desires are still a moral muddle, all mixed up between healthy desire for my wife and unhealthy attractions to others or to top-shelf magazines and so on. That is not a remarkable confession that warrants a place in the tabloids ('Church minister confesses to lust – shock, horror!'); it is just the way it is for all of us, one way or another. We need to remember that the Bible is addressed to those who are sexually spoiled.

Jesus Christ offers forgiveness and restoration to those with spoiled sexual pasts

'Neither do I condemn you; go, and . . . sin no more.'
(John 8:11)

The second basic truth is this: the good news of Jesus Christ offers forgiveness to those whose sexual pasts are spoiled.

Sexual sin is not the unforgivable sin, and sexual damage is not irreparable. Whatever we may have done, seen, or thought, and whatever may have been done to us, the Bible speaks to us 'the word of [God's] grace' (Acts 20:32). The Bible is peppered with signs of this grace. The families of Abraham, Isaac, and Jacob were dysfunctional in the extreme, yet the promised line to Christ went through them. King David committed adultery and then arranged for the woman's husband to be killed in battle; yet he turned from his wrongdoing and was forgiven (2 Samuel 11 – 12; Psalm 51). The woman with whom he committed adultery is even given a special mention in the family tree of Jesus Christ (Matthew 1:6)!

Although people often expect the church to condemn those who have got it wrong in the area of sex, the reverse ought to be the case. We are to follow in the footsteps of Jesus, who brings new life to a woman with a deeply troubled past (John 4:1–42) and speaks forgiveness to a woman caught in the very act of adultery (John 8:1–11). Prostitutes were drawn to him by the attractiveness of his purity and the offer of his forgiveness (e.g. Luke 7:36–50). Indeed, it was the sexual failures who entered the kingdom of God ahead of those who thought they were clean (Matthew 21:31–32). It was the Pharisees who tied up heavy burdens of religious obligation and put them on people's shoulders, making the whole religion thing hard to bear (Matthew 23:4). The Lord Jesus, by contrast, will not break a bruised reed or snuff out a weakly flickering candle (Matthew 12:20, quoting Isaiah 42:1–4). His yoke is easy and his burden is light (Matthew 11:29–30). So whatever our pasts, our thoughts, our desires, perhaps also our actions and wrong relationships, Jesus Christ offers you and me forgiveness and grace.

> I will restore to you the years
>   that the . . . locust has eaten . . .
> (Joel 2:25)

This forgiveness and restoration is beautifully pictured in an Old Testament prophecy in the prophet Joel. My wife and I were trying to help a dear friend whose life was plagued by the memory of a sexual sin. She had turned from it long ago, but somehow the memory still troubled her. Nothing we could say seemed to help, until my wife turned her to this prophecy. It was given to a people whose land and lives had been ravaged by a plague of locusts in punishment for their sin. They knew it was their fault, and they repented. But they must have despaired of their lives ever being restored. 'We have gone too far, got too messed up, blown our chances,' they must have thought.

And then they heard this word from God: 'I will restore to you the years that the swarming locust has eaten, the hopper, the destroyer, and the cutter' (Joel 2:25). This verse is an Old Testament preaching of the gospel and an anticipation of the promise of Christ. However spoiled and ravaged your life may be in the area of sex, if you will turn to Christ he promises to restore to you the years that the locust has eaten. This will not necessarily mean sexual fulfilment in this life, although it may well include a real measure of healing and restoration. But it will most certainly mean something deeper: a full and free forgiveness and a fresh start. And in the age to come, it will mean a satisfaction and fulfilment which will leave the best sex in the universe in the shade (see Conclusion, page 165)!

God's grace enables us to live lives of purity

[11]For the grace of God has appeared, bringing salvation for all people, [12]*training us to renounce ungodliness and worldly passions, and to live self-controlled, upright, and godly lives in the present age,* [13]waiting for our blessed hope, the appearing of the glory of our great God and Saviour Jesus Christ, [14]who gave himself for us to

redeem us from all lawlessness and *to purify for himself* a people
for his own possession who are zealous for good works.
(Titus 2:11–14, author's emphases)

The third basic truth moves us on from forgiveness. It is this:
the God who graciously forgives us also acts powerfully within
us to change us. God does not just forgive us and then leave us
to get on as we did before, which was not very well. Instead he
places his Spirit, his own presence, in our hearts as his personal
power to invade, cleanse and reshape our spoiled hearts. As
Paul says to his colleague Titus in the Bible passage above, the
grace of God *trains* us to renounce ungodliness and worldly
passions, and to live new lives. Jesus came *to purify for himself* a
people for his own possession who are zealous for good works.

Whatever our stories, we must never underestimate the
power of grace to train and purify. After giving that terrible list
of sins to the church in Corinth, Paul goes on to say, 'And such
were some of you. *But* you were washed, you were sanctified
[set apart to live differently now], you were justified in the
name of the Lord Jesus Christ and by the Spirit of our God'
(1 Corinthians 6:9–11).

Years ago, I remember reading one of those pop-psychology
books that was a best-seller at the time. Those books always
depress me, because they say, more or less, that if this or that
happened in childhood, then these bad effects will be seen in
adulthood. As I read I usually find myself feeling first, that
my parents made some of these mistakes in my childhood (as
all parents do – though in fact mine were terrific!), and second,
that I in turn seem to have made all these mistakes with my
own children in their childhood. There would seem to be no
hope for any of us. But I vividly remember the comment of a
good friend as we discussed the book. 'The trouble with that
book', he said, 'is that it leaves no room for grace.' How right
he was. The grace of God can come into the most deeply
broken life and bring cleansing, and then that same grace can

train a cleansed life to become a life of growing purity. That is as true in the area of sex as in every other area of human life.

So, as we study the Bible together, never forget that it speaks to those with spoiled and damaged histories, to whom Jesus Christ offers forgiveness and restoration. And never forget that by his grace God can turn a spoiled life into a life of growing purity which will be perfected when he gives us resurrection bodies at the end.

For study or discussion

Read again the passages printed in this chapter (1 Corinthians 6:9–11, John 8:11, Joel 2:25, and Titus 2:11–14).

1. Who have most influenced you by their examples (good or bad) in the area of sex and marriage? Think both about people you have known and characters you have seen portrayed in movies, soaps, magazines or books.

2. Describe these role models, whether good or bad. How have these people behaved, and what have you learned from them (positive or negative)?

3. How have they influenced your thinking about what is right and wrong?

4. If you are (or may one day be) married, what kind of 'baggage' do you think you bring into marriage, in your thinking and your expectations?

5. Pause to bring this 'baggage' quietly before God. Pray through the truths of grace in this chapter and ask God to put them deep in your heart. Claim the forgiveness and cleansing of Christ for your past.

6. What are your areas of struggle in the area of sexual purity? How do you think you can move forward, by the grace of God? Pray for grace to grow in purity in the future.

2 Married for a purpose

Laura felt lonely and bitter. She and Andy had been married for four years now. She thought back to their wedding day, which had been amazing. The vicar had given an inspiring talk from Genesis, where God says, 'It is not good for a man to be alone.' Her heart had warmed as he had described her and Andy as being in a kind of fairy-tale; how in his love God had made them for each other; how it was not good for them to be on their own and lonely; and how now they were married they would never again need to be lonely. Wow! She had loved that. All those longings – about to be fulfilled with Andy. Her heart was all a-flutter as she was swept along by the magic of the day.

But now, four hard years later, she sat and wept tears of self-pity and bitterness. How could the reality be so different? After their wedding, she and Andy had moved to a different city, following Andy's job relocation. All Laura's university friends were miles away now. And even though her phone bill was astronomical, she felt very lonely. Andy was busy and absorbed in work, but still seemed to expect her to be all smiles when he came home in the evening (usually an hour and a half after she finished her much duller job – she'd not been able to get a job suited to her training).

To be honest, marriage for Laura was really not all it had been cracked up to be. It really didn't match the description on the tin, or not the description given her by that vicar. And in her bitterness she wondered if there was really any point in keeping it all going, if the rest of her life was going to be like this. What *was* the point?

Well, what *is* the point? Let us go right back to basics: why did God make human beings male and female? When Christian people have searched the Bible, they have come up with three answers.

1. *Children rather than barrenness*: sex is in order to have children, and children are a good thing.
2. *Faithfulness rather than selfishness*: sex is for faithful intimacy, and intimate relationship is a good thing.
3. *Order rather than chaos*: marriage guards sexual desires from destroying society, so that society does not descend into sexual chaos.

These three are sometimes called the traditional 'goods' (i.e. 'good purposes') of marriage. Each finds support in the Bible, and chapters 3, 4 and 6 will explore them further. But the problem with coming up with three separate answers is that we are not sure which is more important than which. In particular, Roman Catholics usually emphasize that having children is the number one purpose, whereas Protestants are more likely to major on the marriage relationship. And no one is very enthusiastic about the third, because somehow it feels rather negative!

But how are we to decide? On which of these goals ought we

to focus in our marriages? What is the point, for a Laura who is struggling with a lonely marriage? Why keep going? Or what is the point for a couple who are denied the gift of children (as indeed a very significant minority of grieving couples are)? Does this make their marriage empty and pointless? We need one unifying purpose of God to hold our thinking together. That is, we need to know God's big 'point' for making us male and female.

So in this chapter, which is the foundation of our study, I want to go back to Genesis and ask the really fundamental question of why God chose to make humankind male and female. When Jesus was asked about sex and marriage he went back to Genesis 1 and 2 for his authority; Paul did the same. These two chapters are God's way of telling us what we need to know about the shape of the universe before it was spoiled.

Two passages in Genesis 1 and 2 lay the foundations for marriage: Genesis 1:26–31 and Genesis 2:15–25. Jesus and Paul quote from both Genesis 1:27 ('male and female he created them') and Genesis 2:24 ('Therefore a man shall leave his father and his mother and hold fast to his wife, and they shall become one flesh'). We can find these quotations in Mark 10:6–8, Ephesians 5:31, and 1 Corinthians 6:16. We must look carefully at both these foundational passages in Genesis.

Foundations in Genesis 1:26–31

26Then God said, 'Let us make man in our image, after our likeness. And let them have dominion over the fish of the sea and over the birds of the heavens and over the livestock and over all the earth and over every creeping thing that creeps on the earth.'

27So God created man in his own image,
    in the image of God he created him;
    male and female he created them.

[28]And God blessed them. And God said to them, 'Be fruitful and multiply and fill the earth and subdue it and have dominion over the fish of the sea and over the birds of the heavens and over every living thing that moves on the earth.' [29]And God said, 'Behold, I have given you every plant yielding seed that is on the face of all the earth, and every tree with seed in its fruit. You shall have them for food. [30]And to every beast of the earth and to every bird of the heavens and to everything that creeps on the earth, everything that has the breath of life, I have given every green plant for food.' And it was so. [31]And God saw everything that he had made, and behold, it was very good. And there was evening and there was morning, the sixth day.
(Genesis 1:26–31)

Genesis 1 describes almost poetically the creation of a world which is repeatedly called 'good' (verses 4, 10, 12, 18, 25). But in verse 26 something happens which turns it from 'good' into 'very good' (verse 31). This something brings to completion the work of creation, so that after this God can look at the finished work and pronounce it 'very good'. This climax to creation is the making of men and women. The reason this is so very good is that men and women are going to govern and care for God's world and keep it an ordered place, full of life.

Verses 26–31 teach or imply four closely related things about human beings.

- First, we are made in the image and likeness of God. We have a unique dignity not shared by animals or plants.
- Second, we are entrusted with a unique privilege. We are to fill the earth with men and women who will care for it.
- Third, we are created male and female. We are to use our maleness and femaleness to care for God's world.

- And fourth, we are to rejoice in our Creator. This is implied in Genesis, and spelt out in Psalm 8. We are to live in thankful dependence on God and cheerful obedience to his command.

These four truths, of dignity, privilege, sexuality, and joy before God, are to be held closely together. When we think about marriage, we need to think about God, and our privilege of caring for his world. I like to sum this up with the motto *sex in the service of God*. Like all mottos, this simplifies my point. I do not mean to suggest that marriage is only about sex. But it is sex that distinguishes marriage from any other friendship or partnership. By 'sex' in this motto, I mean a shorthand for the whole of marriage as it develops and grows out of its heart and core of sexual intimacy and faithfulness. Sex is shorthand for the marriage relationship in all its fullness: in intimacy, friendship, partnership, fun and faithfulness. The motto is to remind us that the whole business of marriage in all its fullness is to be lived in the loving joyful service of God, as we look outwards from our marriages and as couples seek to care for God's world together. (Unmarried people are also called to rejoice in God and serve him in his world, but there are particular and distinctive ways in which married people can do this.)

In the drama of Genesis 1, by the time we reach verse 25 the world is teeming with all kinds of living creatures. If human beings are to govern this abundant world, there need to be lots of us; hence 'male and female' and the blessing of multiplication. We are male and female so that we may use our maleness and femaleness in joyful service of God in the government of his world.

That sets the scene. But what about Genesis 2, where the drama is told in terms of the garden in Eden? Does this give a conflicting picture? Many think it does. I want to show you why it matters to understand it rightly.

Foundations in Genesis 2:15–25

[15]The LORD God took the man and put him in the garden of Eden to work it and keep it. [16]And the LORD God commanded the man, saying, 'You may surely eat of every tree of the garden, [17]but of the tree of the knowledge of good and evil you shall not eat, for in the day that you eat of it you shall surely die.'

[18]Then the LORD God said, 'It is not good that the man should be alone; I will make him a helper fit for him.' [19]So out of the ground the LORD God formed every beast of the field and every bird of the heavens and brought them to the man to see what he would call them. And whatever the man called every living creature, that was its name. [20]The man gave names to all livestock and to the birds of the heavens and to every beast of the field. But for Adam there was not found a helper fit for him. [21]So the LORD God caused a deep sleep to fall upon the man, and while he slept took one of his ribs and closed up its place with flesh. [22]And the rib that the LORD God had taken from the man he made into a woman and brought her to the man. [23]Then the man said,

'This at last is bone of my bones
    and flesh of my flesh;
she shall be called Woman,
    because she was taken out of Man.'

[24]Therefore a man shall leave his father and his mother and hold fast to his wife, and they shall become one flesh. [25]And the man and his wife were both naked and were not ashamed.
(Genesis 2:15–25)

How Genesis 2:18 is wrongly understood

Let me first tell you how Genesis 2:18 has often been understood, and then show you that this is wrong. In verse 18 God says, 'It is not good that the man should be alone; I will make him a helper fit for him.' This is very striking. In the world which we have been repeatedly told is 'good', and finally 'very good', there is something 'not good': that is, until the creation of the woman to be the helper to the man. The question is, what is 'not good'? The answer is, 'that the man should be alone'. But what does 'alone' mean?

It is very common to take 'alone' to mean 'lonely'. 'Ah,' we say, 'poor Adam was lonely. There he is in the garden surrounded by animals. But a pet dog, cat, ox, budgerigar or goldfish does not meet his relational needs. God will give him a wife so that he will not be lonely any more.'

It is very common to read it like this. One writer says that God is simply filling Adam's 'personal need'; another that 'the reason for marriage is to solve the problem of loneliness.' I was reading a children's Bible story book to our daughter some years ago. We had come to Genesis 24. Here, the elderly Abraham wants to make sure his promised son Isaac marries someone from within his own people. He is concerned about the proper continuation of the promised family line. But my rewritten Bible story book tells me that Abraham thought to himself, 'I must make sure that Isaac has a wife to love him. I don't want him to be on his own when I die' (my italics). But Genesis 24 does not say this! This is how twenty-first-century people understand it: that unless I am married I will not be loved, and unless I am married I am bound to be lonely.

The motto for this misunderstanding might be sex for the fulfilment of me or sex in the service of us. My concern is my fulfilment, sex to meet my needs. However, it is a mistake to think that Genesis 2:18 ('It is not good for the man to be alone') means that marriage is created to meet my needs. There are two reasons why this is wrong, and a further two why it is disastrous in its results.

Why marriage is not the answer to loneliness

Reason 1: Genesis 2:18 must be read in its context

First, it is false because it takes the verse out of its context in the story of Genesis 2. Verse 18 does not come out of the blue, but is part of a drama that begins in verse 4. Right at the start of this second telling of the creation story, there is a problem: that there is no man to work the ground, to farm it (verse 5).

So, naturally, God makes a man to do just that, to care for his world (verse 7). This is what human beings are for, as we learned in Genesis 1:26–28. So he puts the man in the garden and gives him his orders (verse 15), which are 'to work [the garden] and keep [or guard] it'. That is, Adam is to be the gardener or park-keeper, with the enormous responsibility and dignity of being entrusted with God's garden.

In this context, God takes a good look at the garden and at little Adam standing bemused in the middle of it and says, 'I can see that it is not good for him to be given this job on his own.' It is not good, not because he is lonely (he may or may not be!), but quite simply because the job is too big for him to do on his own. This is why he is given 'a helper' rather than 'a companion'. If he was lonely, then a companion would be what he needed, to sit with him on the garden bench, to hold hands, and so on. But although no doubt Eve would have been a splendid companion (and a wife *is* called a 'companion' in Malachi 2:14), she is given him here as his 'helper', which simply means one who works alongside so that both together can do the task.

It is worth asking why, when Adam needed a helper, God chose to make the woman, rather than another man. For, at risk of seeming either trivial or politically incorrect, we would have to admit that purely in terms of averages, another male might have been stronger! So why the woman?

Genesis 1 and 2 suggest two reasons. Genesis 1 suggests that it is to do with having children (1:28). This makes perfect sense. For if one gardener is not enough for such a great garden, nor will two be. They need to start a whole family of gardeners!

But Genesis 2 adds another reason, which is the delight of sexual intimacy. In verse 23 Adam responds to seeing Eve with a rapturous cry of delight: 'This at last . . . !' At last here is the one who is the answer to his longing for a helper suitable for him, to work alongside him in delightful fellowship in the privilege of serving God in the garden.

Adam's cry of delight in Genesis 2:23 has been echoed by bridegrooms down the ages. There is here (as in verse 25) a natural 'Yes!' to sexual desire and delight untouched by shame. But even here the context makes us remember that the final goal is not the delight of sexual intimacy. For this is delight with a shared purpose, intimacy with a common goal, and companionship in a task that stretches beyond the boundaries of the couple themselves. As we rejoice with the lovers in the garden, we must not forget that there is work to be done. The garden needs gardening. God's world needs watchful care and careful work. Those who are single will serve in many fruitful ways possible only for the unattached. But for those who are married, this work will be done together as a couple. So the motto for marriage in Genesis 2 is the same as the motto in Genesis 1: *sex in the service of God*.

It is important also to mention that gardening (in this imagery) is not restricted to married men and women. The unmarried person is called to serve God in his world every bit as much. My point is simply that, if or when we marry, that calling to serve God does not cease. Far from it; it simply changes the ways in which we serve him. A married couple contribute to 'the work of the garden' in certain distinctive ways, which are explored in chapters 3, 4 and 6.

Reason 2: The rest of the Bible does not support the theory
The second reason it is a mistake to think marriage is fundamentally God's remedy for loneliness is that the rest of the Bible does not teach this. If Genesis 2:18 did teach this, we might reasonably expect the rest of the Bible to say the same.

What we find is a resounding silence. The Bible says a great deal about the longings of the human heart. But these longings are not necessarily to be fulfilled in marriage; rather they are to be satisfied through fellowship, a walking together with our fellow human beings. Above all, we are all (married or single) made for joyful fellowship with the God who loves us. And we are made also for warm fellowship with our brothers and sisters in the family of God. This is what the gospel of Jesus Christ offers to everyone.

Now marriage ought also to be a place of friendship and joyful fellowship. For those who are married, their marriages ought indeed to be places of fellowship which are remedies for loneliness. But marriage is not *the* remedy for loneliness. Wherever there is fellowship there is God's remedy for loneliness. Not all human beings are able to marry, but all human beings are invited into fellowship with God and with one another in Jesus Christ.

It is worth studying some of the great Bible passages about love, and seeing how, for the most part, they have nothing to do with sex and marriage and everything to do with God and his people. Of course there are exceptions, notably the Song of Songs. But consider these examples:

- In 1 John 4:7–21 John writes warmly both of the love of God and of love for one another, but marriage is nowhere in sight.
- In 1 Thessalonians 2:6–8 Paul writes with great passion about his love for these Christians, but again sex and marriage are nowhere in view.
- In John 13 – 16 Jesus speaks with touching intimacy of his friendship with his disciples and their love for one another, yet, again, he is not talking about sex and marriage at all.
- In particular, please note that the wonderful description of love in 1 Corinthians 13 has nothing whatever to do

with marriage, but everything to do with the love that ought to be present in a church fellowship (but wasn't present in Corinth!).

- Even the Psalms, which are so full of the whole breadth of human emotion and longing, scarcely mention marriage (except for the royal wedding in Psalm 45). When the 'solitary' are mentioned in Psalm 68:6, God's kindness puts them in a 'home' or 'family', not necessarily into a marriage but into a family. And the greatest family is the people of God.

For these two reasons, the context of Genesis 2 and the teaching of the rest of the Bible, we can see that Genesis 2:18 does not teach that the purpose of marriage is to remedy loneliness. Rather, the motto in Genesis 2 is still *sex in the service of God*. The man and the woman go out into the garden to work together. God's purpose for marriage is that those who are married serve him in and through their marriages (just as those who are single serve him in their singleness).

So we see that marriage is not God's answer for loneliness. Indeed, marriage is not God's provision to meet your or my needs. We would like to think that it was. But God has bigger purposes in the world than meeting our needs. This reminds me of one of my favourite cartoons, in which a group of cavemen stand on top of a cliff, watching one of their number fall over the edge. He has evidently just been thrown off the top. As he falls, the leader of the group (who has thrown the offender off) looks round angrily at the others and asks, 'Well, is there anyone else here whose needs are not being met?' This cartoon is a mischievous but timely critique of a culture in which we expect everything, including our marriages, to meet our needs.

When we approach marriage expecting our needs to be met, we have not understood the real nature of love, and we are sowing the seeds of destruction in our marriages.

Why 'marriage to meet my needs' is wrong
Because it is not real love

> If you love those who love you, what benefit is that to you? For
> even sinners love those who love them.
> (Luke 6:32)

First, inward-looking marriage is not real love because it
encourages us to view sex and marriage selfishly. Jesus teaches
'If you love those who love you, what credit is that to you?'
(Luke 6:32). Any love that simply gazes adoringly into the eyes
of another who adores us is not really love at all. For genuine
love always overflows to others.

One of the most frightening things about Jesus' parable of
the rich man and Lazarus (Luke 16:19–31) is that the rich man
seems to have been a good family man. Even in the place of the
dead he is concerned for his brothers. But his so-called love is
not really love at all, for it never extends to the poor man
Lazarus who lies at his gate. He cares for his family, but his care
does not overflow to needy people outside. Marriage and
family can easily become just a respectable form of selfishness.
If we marry mainly to meet our own needs, then our marriages
will be just that: good-looking masks for selfishness.

It is a short step from 'loving you' to 'loving me and wanting
you'. It is too easy for Christians to think of marriage as a
discipleship-free zone. So that outside of marriage we talk
about sacrifice, taking up our cross and so on. But inside
marriage we just talk about how to communicate better, how
to be more intimate, how to have better sex, how to be happy.
One speaker in a church debate spoke of her desire for her sons
to find 'a marriage of openness, intimacy, sexual fulfilment and
the pursuit of personal significance'. Instead we should want
marriages that serve God. If they are sexually and personally
fulfilled, well and good. But if they do not serve God, no
amount of personal fulfilment will make them right. After all,

so far as we can see, Ananias and Sapphira had a marriage with excellent communication and shared values; each understood the other perfectly; and yet they died terrible deaths under the judgment of God (Acts 5:1–11).

Because it destroys marriages
Second, a self-centred view of sex and marriage destroys marriage and society. Just as we have higher than ever expectations of what marriage will give us, so at the same time marriages break down as never before.

We can see this destructiveness by looking at how societies work. Societies in which sex and marriage are viewed as a means to personal fulfilment encourage a man and a woman to gaze soft-focus into each other's eyes, and encourage each to find in the other all they need, each to be all to the other. Such cultures promote what we may call a 'religion of coupledom', in which the goal of every man and woman must be to live in such an exquisite union. The very word 'relationship', when used as shorthand for 'sexual relationship', shows this way of thinking. To be outside 'relationship' is presumably to be lonely. And if it were true that 'relationship' is to be found primarily in *sexual* relationship, then we would have to seek such sexual intimacy at all costs. We do not need to swallow this lie, for relationship has nothing *necessarily* to do with sex and marriage.

Cynics say of the weather in the west of Scotland that, if you cannot see the mountains, it is raining; and if you *can* see the mountains, it is about to rain! Likewise in popular dramas, the lead characters are either in sexual relationships or about to be (or, if not, then it's not a 'feel-good' movie and probably fails at the box office!). When did we last see a successful movie which portrayed a contented bachelor or spinster? The very words have negative connotations!

But this focus on the couple isolates them from the supportive influences of wider family and society. The defining moment is thought to be when they are alone in the bedroom, not when they serve together as a new social and family unit in the wider society. Sociologists have noted how destructively intense such relationships become, and therefore how brief. The historian Lawrence Stone writes, 'It is an ironic thought that just at the moment when some thinkers are heralding the advent of the perfect marriage based on full satisfaction of the sexual, emotional, and creative needs of both husband and wife, the proportion of marital breakdowns . . . is rising rapidly.' Christopher Brooke, another historian, writes, 'While faced with the spectacle of broken marriages, we have come (by a strange paradox which however goes very deep into the roots of the subject) to expect far more from a happy marriage.' But, as one theologian put it, 'even the smallest cottage of the happiest of lovers cannot be habitable unless it has at least a door and a few windows opening outwards.'

For we were not made to gaze forever into the eyes of another human being and find in him or her all we need. And if we think we were, then we are bound to be disappointed. If my dear wife ever thought I could be everything to her, then she certainly knows better now! And, of course, if I think marriage is there to meet my needs, what do I do when it fails to meet them? One writer says that, on this basis, 'I have a *moral obligation* to divorce and seek a new mate if my original one can no longer promote my growth and self-actualisation' (my emphasis).

This irony, that we expect so much of marriage but find it disappointing, is an irony the Bible understands perfectly. It calls it idolatry. This means that if I pursue any goal except the honour of God, then I am worshipping an idol. And idols are empty, vacuous, disappointing things that have no power to help me. We see this brilliantly exposed in Isaiah 44:9–20 and in Psalm 135:15–18. The moment I make my 'relationship' the goal of my life I doom myself to disappointment. Surprisingly, the key to a good marriage is not to pursue a good marriage, but to pursue the honour of God. We need to replace this selfish model of marriage with one in which we work side by side in God's 'garden' (that is, God's world), rather than gaze for ever into each other's eyes.

What difference does a spoiled world make to serving God?

We have studied the foundations in Genesis 1 and 2 and summed up our findings in the motto *sex in the service of God*. But we cannot read straight from those foundational chapters to the world as it is. Between Genesis 1 and 2 and the rest of the Bible lies Genesis 3, in which the man and the woman disobey God and the whole world comes under the curse. The 'gardeners' rebel and become vandals, which is why the world is in such a mess. At the heart of the curse is creation no longer ruled by men and women who are lovingly responsible to the Creator. This is why creation groans and longs for the children of God to come and rule it as they ought (Romans 8:19–22).

So it is not enough to say that we ought to serve God in our marriages. We need to be forgiven before we can serve. Otherwise we will simply be recruiting more vandals into the 'garden'. Until I am put right with God through Jesus Christ, I do not know the Creator God and have not begun to walk lovingly before him, with a grasp of how he governs the world and therefore how I ought to care for it. I need to be transformed from vandalism to horticulture; to be made by grace a 'gardener' before I can do the 'gardening'.

Adam and Eve were told to 'be fruitful and multiply' (Genesis 1:28). God wanted a growing team of 'gardeners'. But after the great disobedience of Genesis 3, more human beings does not automatically mean more good 'gardeners'. It may simply mean more vandals! So what we need now is not just more people, but people who are brought back into the family of God, to know and love God and therefore to become good 'gardeners'. This is why Abraham, the head of the family of faith, is given a repeat of the 'multiplication' promise originally given to Adam (e.g. Genesis 15:5; 17:4). The rest of the human race does multiply, but blessing comes to the world through the multiplication of God's people, because they are (or ought to be) trained to be 'gardeners'.

This means that serving God today cannot be done simply by having children. We need first and foremost to proclaim the good news of Jesus Christ and to call on people to bow the knee to him. So, throughout this book, when we speak of the service of God, we must remember that proclaiming Jesus Christ is at the forefront of that service.

Conclusion: sex is for the service of God

I finish this chapter, as I ended the introduction, with a call to repent. Each of us by nature seeks our own happiness and self-satisfaction. We do this in the area of sex as much as in every other area of life. By nature our motto will always be 'sex in the service of us'.

We have been created male and female not to satisfy our needs, but to serve our Creator. He has put us in charge of his good world, and he wants our maleness and femaleness to be used in the service of that world. This is true for those who are not married, who are to serve him joyfully and fruitfully as unmarried men and women. But for those who are married it means we must ask the question: 'How does God want us to serve him together in our marriage? How can our motto become *sex in the service of God*?'

This does not necessarily mean that husband and wife must always be in the same place doing exactly the same work. Mostly this won't be possible. What it means is that each is supporting the other as best they can, so that between them, both apart and together, they serve God in and through their marriage.

To do this will have very practical implications for how they earn and spend money, for how lifestyle decisions reflect the values of the kingdom of God, and for giving.

If you are single, and perhaps would love to be married but the opportunity has not arisen, ask God to help you not to live your life in a kind of suspended animation, waiting for your prince or princess to come along. Resolve afresh to serve him with joy and contentment in your current state.

If you are preparing for marriage, ask God to help you and your partner to make it your aim to serve him wholeheartedly in marriage. If you are married, rededicate yourselves as a couple to the service of God. Turn your eyes away from the practical matters of how well you communicate, how good sex is, how well you care for each other (all of which are important), and realign yourselves with the God who made you. Make it your prayer to serve him in his world with all the resources and opportunities that your marriage provides. Chapters 3, 4 and 6 will explore three ways in which married couples distinctively can do just that.

For study or discussion

Read Genesis 1 and 2 right through.

1. What are the three traditional Christian answers to the question 'What is the point of marriage?'

2. a. What four truths does Genesis 1:26–31 teach about human beings?

b. How do these help us understand God's purpose for sex and marriage?

c. What motto is suggested?

3. a. How has Genesis 2:18 been misunderstood?

b. How do we know this is wrong?

4. Why is this misunderstanding of Genesis 2:18 disastrous?

5. What does Genesis 2:18 really mean and how does this help us understand God's purpose for marriage?

6. Examine your attitude to marriage (whether or not you are married). How can you (re)align your attitude and aims with God's purpose?

7. Talk honestly about your attitudes to money. Read 1 Timothy 6:6–10, 17–19; James 5:1–6; Luke 12:13–21.
   a. Are you happy that you earn money in a way that honours God; that is just and fair?

   b. What standard of living have you been used to (perhaps in your childhood)?

c. What expectations do you bring with you into marriage?

d. Do you expect a steadily rising standard of living?

e. What happens when you put these expectations under the microscope and look at them from the perspective of serving God in his world?

f. Are you open with each other about money?

g. Do you have the same priorities, and are they God's priorities?

h. What do you do (or will you do) about giving as a couple?

8. If you have been married for some time, review how your marriage is serving God.
   a. Have your circumstances changed, for example with the birth of children, or children leaving home?

   b. How can you serve God in these changed circumstances?

9. How will serving God affect decisions about jobs?

3 What is the point of having children?

Garry put the phone down, stunned. He had not expected this. He and Sarah had been married just six months. And Sarah was pregnant. Really he had not expected this. They hadn't talked about children, and certainly hadn't planned on having a family just yet. And now she was pregnant. Within a few seconds his mind had swept through (a) the mortgage and how it relied on Sarah's salary, (b) the planned trekking holiday in six months' time, (c) the size of their one-bedroom flat, and (d) a host of other implications, all unwelcome.

When he arrived home, he found Sarah in floods of tears. She had been worrying about whether she had it in her to be a good mother, and had persuaded herself she never could be. She was frightened. Garry didn't really try to comfort her. Instead they had a row about whose 'fault' it was.

When the news leaked out at work, Garry's and Sarah's respective colleagues offered their congratulations. 'Commiserations, more like!' was all they could think, though they put a brave face on it. 'Yes, we're very pleased,' said

Garry and Sarah through gritted teeth. But inside they wondered what on earth was the big deal? To them it just seemed like a most unfortunate accident.

And God blessed them. And God said to them, 'Be fruitful and multiply and fill the earth and subdue it and have dominion over the fish of the sea and over the birds of the heavens and over every living thing that moves on the earth.'
(Genesis 1:28)

We have seen in chapter 2 that God made us male and female so that we might serve him in caring for his world. I suggested the motto *sex in the service of God*. In this chapter and chapters 4 and 6 we work out what this means in practice, taking the three traditional reasons for marriage: children, relationship, and sexual order.

Although it may seem counter-cultural, we are going to begin with children. This may seem as unwelcome to the reader as the pregnancy was to Sarah and Garry. But this is quite deliberate. If you are engaged or wondering whether to get engaged, it may seem a bit premature to start talking about children. After all, they seem a long way ahead! But I want to suggest to you that if you are thinking about marriage, you need to think now about children and where they fit into God's picture. So please don't skip this chapter.

For childless couples this is bound to be a painful chapter. It will hurt as you read of God's purpose for children in marriage, and I am sorry about that. I very much hope that the section on childlessness towards the end of the chapter will be of some comfort and help to you.

In Genesis 1:28 we saw that the blessing 'be fruitful and multiply' is given so that men and women will be able to govern and care for the world God has entrusted to them. We serve God by bringing up children in the hope that they too will in turn serve God. In Genesis 2 we deduced the same point using the language of the 'garden'. The job of caring for the garden was too big for Adam the gardener to do on his own (Genesis 2:15, 18), and so Eve is given to work alongside him as his helper. Alongside her contributions to the work (as an equal human being alongside Adam), it is her unique privilege to bear and nurture children and so increase the 'gardening' team.

Children are a blessing not a curse

The Bible therefore understands children to be a blessing rather than a curse. It consistently affirms what it poetically calls 'blessings of the breasts and of the womb' (Genesis 49:25), rejoices at birth and laments when birth is interrupted by death. This Old Testament attitude became one of the ways in which the early church was most clearly different from the society of its day. One of the things that made the early Christians stand out most strikingly from their contemporaries was their refusal to accept abortion or infanticide (especially the killing of baby daughters, which was – and still is, in parts of the world – common). They were deeply pro-life and anti-death. We ought to be the same.

This is a deep and fundamental attitude not shared by contemporary Western society. The Bible turns us towards children with thanksgiving to God. But Western society in some ways seems to consider children a curse. This is strong language, but I think it is true. Some trends in society turn us away from children with anxiety and fear. More than one in five conceptions in Britain is terminated by an abortion, many of them within marriage, but far more outside marriage (for a cohabiting couple, abortion is about four times more likely than for a married couple). For decades now we have been having children on average later in life (about a year later for each decade from 1970 onwards), and having fewer children in our families. Since the 1970s the birthrate in most European countries has been well below that needed to keep the population steady. Were it not for immigration, we would be like Japan, where the population is even set to fall in absolute terms. (In other parts of the world, of course, we have the reverse problem: attitudes to children are very positive, and there may be a case for encouraging slower population growth.)

Without God's perspective, children tend either to be idolized (if they are adorable) or abused (if they are not). Some people don't want them at all. So the chairman of the British Association of Non-Parents (i.e. deliberate non-parents) says, 'I have never wanted to be a father. I have never wanted that sort of responsibility. It is the fact that child-rearing goes on every bloody day for so long . . . I just do not want to devote myself in this way to children.' He is right about the demands of parenting, but wrong to be so selfish. A counsellor with the marriage counselling service Relate comments that the decision not to have children is 'usually a lifestyle thing. They have a life they enjoy and feel that children would change it too much.'

Of course many people still do want children. Even here, however, the world's perspective is often different from the Bible's. So, for example, some people may choose to have children because they need to be needed, like the actress Michelle Pfeiffer, who said, 'I'm one of those people who needed to have children. I needed to have that centre to my life, that base.' Some want to have children when they choose, of the gender that they want, with the genes that they prefer. The decision to have children or not is viewed as just a personal lifestyle choice. But the Bible gives us a very different picture. Children are a wonderful gift of God and we should be deeply thankful for them, however exhausting and troublesome they may sometimes be!

We are to nurture children so they learn to serve God

The Bible's perspective is that we ought to want children in marriage because we want to serve God. The blessing of children is an important practical way in which a married couple can serve God in their marriage. Fundamentally we are to desire children neither because we find them adorable (if we do), nor because others expect us to have children (if they do), but because we understand that this is how God populates his 'garden' with 'gardeners' to care for it. The Creator entrusts to married couples the awesome privilege and responsibility of pro-creating (creating on his behalf) potential gardeners to join his team.

Parenting is therefore very important. None of us gets it right, and we must always leave room for the grace of God. But it is very important. It is not enough that baby potential 'gardeners' are born. We are to work, teach, discipline, and pray that they will grow into adult actual 'gardeners', who learn to love God and care for his world. We are told that it was God's will for Abraham 'that he may *command his children and his household after him* to keep the way of the LORD by doing righteousness and justice' (Genesis 18:19, my emphasis).

Having children goes far beyond the sometimes rather straightforward and enjoyable business of conceiving a child. It is not enough to conceive a child, for a child to grow in the womb and be safely born, even to be physically fed and watered so as to grow strong in body. All this is good. But what God wants is 'gardeners', servants who will walk through life with him, and for his sake care for his world.

This means that the whole privilege and enterprise of godly nurture is a vital way in which most married couples use sex in the service of God. It has been said by some wit that 'literature is mostly about sex and hardly ever about children; in real marriage it is pretty much the reverse, mostly about children and frustratingly little about sex!' And yet the two usually go together as integrated parts of the wonder of marriage.

Indeed, the Bible wants us to hold together the hope of having children with the vision of building a home that will be a fruitful part of God's good world. We see this unified vision, for example, in a kind of photographic negative in the threefold curse of Deuteronomy 28:30, where we read of three linked consequences of disobedience to God by God's covenant people. First, 'You shall become engaged to a woman, but another man shall ravish her.' Second, 'You shall build a house, but you shall not dwell in it.' And third, 'You shall plant a vineyard, but you shall not enjoy its fruit.' This is not the denial of three separate and independent blessings (first, a marriage; second, a house; third, a vineyard), but of one coherent blessing. The marriage, the house, and the vineyard are all part of one vision which is bigger than just a couple. It is a vision of a marriage at the heart of a fruitful home. This home contributes to the fruitful government of God's 'garden'.

The book of Proverbs speaks much about the loving discipline of mothers and fathers (e.g. Proverbs 1:8). The Bible understands the powerful influence both of a good or bad mother and of a good or bad father. For example, we are told that King Ahaziah was a moral dead loss because 'his mother was his counsellor in doing wickedly' (2 Chronicles 22:3). By contrast, Timothy owed much to the good example of his godly mother (and grandmother) (Acts 16:1; 2 Timothy 1:5; 3:15). And Paul has a special word to fathers to bring up their children 'in the discipline and instruction of the Lord [that is, the Lord Jesus]' (Ephesians 6:4).

The principle throughout is that parents ought to be both teachers and examples to their children. They are to be teachers of God's truth. And they are to be examples, modelling godliness in the home as best they can, by the grace of God. They ought to be examples of right behaviour, exercising right authority with fairness and grace, and above all loving with the kind of love that does not spoil but wants the very best for the child (Hebrews 12:7–11).

It is important to be clear, however, that we are to do more than just bring up our children to be responsible members of society. In Israel, they were to be taught about the God who made the world (and therefore about right and wrong) and also about how he rescued his people. In Bible terms, nurture needs to teach both law (right and wrong) and grace (trust in Jesus Christ). For unless we teach them about grace and forgiveness in Jesus, right and wrong will simply be burdensome impositions to be resented. So, above all, parents have the duty and privilege of praying for their children morning by morning, evening by evening, and for that matter at many other times. One of the greatest and most undervalued privileges of being brought up in a Christian home is that you will have been prayed for every day of your life.

Having said this, parents must remember that we cannot live our children's lives for them. We are responsible to God for loving them, teaching them, caring for them, disciplining them and praying for them, as we are able. But we are not finally responsible for their response. Timothy's godly mother and grandmother saw Timothy grow into faith and godliness. But it is sobering to remember that the worst of all the kings of Judah, King Manasseh, was the son of one of the very best, King Hezekiah (2 Kings 18 – 21).

So children are to be desired and welcomed because bringing up children is one of the most clearly distinctive ways in which a married couple can serve God. Far from saying 'Two's company, three's a crowd', parents are to say 'Three's company, and four's company, and five is yet more company . . .', because we love to see the 'garden' cared for by more and more 'gardeners'.

All this has very practical implications for parenting. We live in cultures which make idols out of our children's successes. We idolize education, caring more about their getting into good schools and achieving good exam results than we do about their faith and godliness. Often both parents care more about their own careers than about the loving time-consuming godly nurture of their children. This Bible perspective gives us a challenge to line up *our* desires for our children with *God's* desires, and to make parenting decisions in line with God's priorities.

Do we really still need more children, not just more Christians?

Sometimes Christian people object to this very positive attitude to children. They say it is just an Old Testament perspective. But now, they suggest, what we need is not so much more people as more Christians. The physical process of bringing children to birth is to be replaced, they argue, by the spiritual challenge of praying people into new birth.

It is important to see why this line of argument is wrong. The reason is simple, and it is given by Jesus in Luke 20:36. The Sadducees did not believe in bodily resurrection. They came to Jesus with a clever conundrum about someone who had been widowed and then remarried several times. Whose wife would she be in the resurrection? Jesus explains that in the resurrection there will be no more marriage, because 'they cannot die any more'. That is, very simply, in the age to come there will be no more death, and therefore there will be no more need for the next generation, and therefore no more need for marriage.

But until there is no more death, we need generations of children; and this is what marriage is for. It is true that we also need children to come to new birth, to be born of God spiritually, to be born again. But, to put it bluntly, they cannot be born again until they have been born physically for the first time. P. D. James wrote an unusual novel called *The Children of Men* (now a film). This story conjures up a world in which human fertility has fallen to zero, and the youngest human beings are twenty-one years old. It is a haunting novel with no playgroups, no schools, and no hope (well, there would be no hope unless ... But that would spoil the story!).

When preparing for marriage, a couple need to consider three issues arising from this chapter.

Issue 1: Is it right deliberately not to have children?

No. Some Christians will hold different views on this. But I think the deliberate choice not to have children is nearly always wrong. We have seen that some people make this choice and defend it in terms of their rights. In Christian circles the argument is put differently. Christians will not use the blatantly selfish language of the British Association of Non-Parents. Instead we talk about 'serving God *rather than* having children'. But this is a false choice. For having children and giving years of life to costly prayerful nurture of them is precisely the distinctive means by which most married people do serve God. We do not serve God *rather than* having children; we serve God *by* having children. Never despise the significance of parenthood in the service of God! For many, especially (dare I say it?) mothers, what they do as parents will prove more significant in eternity than the most glittering career in the eyes of the world.

This is a question of lining up our values with God's values. Do we agree with the Bible and face children with arms open in gratitude for the blessing of God, or do we turn our face away from children and count as curse what God calls a blessing? Of course, a child may be an inconvenient blessing. A child will usually be an expensive blessing. A child may and often will be a blessing that takes us well outside our comfort zones and into the arms of grace. A child is usually a blessing that will be accompanied by sleepless nights and many tears. But he or she is a blessing, and we must not forget this. Parents struggling with a demanding or wayward child need to remember to thank God for that son or daughter, even as they pray urgently for grace to care for them faithfully.

One of the great reasons why married couples ought to want children is that they force us to welcome into our circle strangers we have not chosen. Husband and wife have chosen one another. But, however much they may have wanted a baby, they did not choose this baby with these particular characteristics! This baby comes into the family circle as a stranger, to be welcomed whatever his or her character and future. And therefore in parenting we learn to welcome the stranger, the one chosen by God for us to love. And we learn to love them out of love for the God who has entrusted them to us. Someone has commented that the only home it is safe to be born into is a hospitable home which welcomes outsiders into its circle. Children challenge our self-centredness and do us good.

So it seems to me that the lifestyle choice of never having children is not generally open to a Christian couple. There may, however, be rare exceptions on medical grounds, where a couple would welcome children if they could, but recognize that it would be irresponsible to do so.

Issue 2: What if we cannot have children?

The more painful and pressing problem for too many couples, however, is wanting to have children but not being able to do so. This is the second issue I want to raise for those considering marriage. This is much more common than is sometimes realized, affecting at one stage or another perhaps as many as one in seven couples. The pain of childlessness is a unique pain. It has been called by one childless couple 'that strange grief which has no focus for its tears and no object for its love'. There is no date on which such a couple become childless, no funeral anniversary on which to focus grief, no photograph or memory of the son or daughter who never was.

What does the Bible say to such couples, and to the rest of us? To them, it says they are right to feel a sense of loss. They are right to want a child, to count as blessing what God calls a blessing, and to pray for it. Their grief is a proper grief. Again and again in the Bible story, childlessness is a cause of grief, and salvation is expressed by the gift of a child. So, for example, Hannah weeps and weeps in her grief at having no child (1 Samuel 1). It is right for a married couple to be sad if they are not given the gift of children. In the Bible story, at certain special times childless parents are given children: notably Abraham and Sarah, the parents of Isaac, and Zechariah and Elizabeth, the parents of John the Baptist. This does not mean that God promises to answer that prayer for every believer, but it is a sign that in the age to come there will be no such fruitlessness or frustration. So the childless couple are right to grieve.

To the rest of us, the Bible says we should 'weep with those who weep' (Romans 12:15). In the nature of things the inability to have children is a matter to be handled with discretion. Such couples do not usually want the whole world to know and pry into the most intimate part of their life together. But it is a great help if they can find a few trusted friends in whom they can confide, who can sorrow with them and commit themselves to pray for them in their pain and uncertainty.

Also, we need to say to childless couples that fruitful service to God does not depend on having children. Many such couples have a deep sense of failure. They see children at the school gate, children in nurseries, children in the crèche at church. They hear announcements of parenting courses, and they listen to preachers talking about their families. And every one of these can be like an arrow to the heart, a sharp reminder of deep pain. Why has God denied us this? Is it because we are no good? Does this mean that our marriage is to be, in a spiritual sense, a barren and fruitless thing? Would we have done better not to have got married?

All these questions go through their minds. But there is absolutely no spiritual need to feel a failure. The Bible teaches that we ought to love God with all our heart. But beyond that, it suggests that there are many, many different ways in which that loving service is worked out, even within marriage. Some are able to adopt, others to foster children, and many to serve in other ways.

To childless people who honour him, God promises:

> I will give in my house and within my walls
>   a monument and a name
>   better than sons and daughters;
> I will give them an everlasting name
>   that shall not be cut off.
> (Isaiah 56:5)

In Old Testament language in Isaiah 56:5 there is a moving promise to those who cannot have natural children, that if they are faithful to God he will give them 'a monument and a name [that is, good reason to be remembered with gratitude as fruitful and significant people] *better than* sons and daughters ... an everlasting name that shall not be cut off.' Many a childless couple has lived a life of deeper spiritual fruitfulness than many who are parents. It may be through generosity, through loving hospitality, or through prayer and costly Christian service. In all sorts of ways, doors open to them for fruitful work together.

Issue 3: What about contraception?

The final issue I need to raise briefly is contraception. It is well known that the Roman Catholic Church officially prohibits artificial contraception. It is not so widely known that their reasons for doing so come not from the Bible, but from philosophy. *Each act* of sexual intercourse, they say, must be open to the possibility of pregnancy.

The Bible does not teach this. It teaches simply that children should be viewed as a blessing and a gift. Sex within marriage does not consist of isolated 'acts' of sexual union. Rather, sex in marriage is the delightful focal point of a whole lifetime of companionship and shared service, lived together in love. The point is that a couple's marriage *as a whole* ought to welcome and pray for the blessing of children. But as to exactly when, or how many, these are matters of Christian freedom. Each couple make their own decisions before God in freedom, and the rest of us are not to judge them. The important thing with contraception is that it should be part of a lifetime together which is fundamentally turned *towards* the blessing of children, rather than turned *against* (which is, of course, the reason contraception is so often used in other contexts).

Having said this, it is important to be aware that some methods of contraception are considered by some to be very early forms of abortion. (For example, if you are considering using an intra-uterine device, it is worth reading about how it works. Trevor Stammers discusses this in *The Family Guide to Sex and Intimacy*, page 178f.) It is important for Christian people to take careful advice and be sure that the contraceptive methods they may use are ethical.

Conclusion

In conclusion, if you are considering getting married, you will do well to remember that welcoming children is part and parcel of God's plan for marriage. If you regard children as a curse, and don't want them, don't get married! If you are preparing for marriage, it is important to discuss your attitude to children. And not just to discuss, but to bring your attitudes into line with God's attitude. You may want to share your fears and misgivings, your anxieties and concerns. But you will do that because together you want to lay before God this dimension of married life, praying together that in God's good time he will give you this gift and then give you grace to bring children up well. You will also want to discuss the possibility that God may choose not to give you this gift; it is important not to take any gift for granted. I remember one Christian telling me very firmly and confidently that he and his wife had 'decided' (rather than, more humbly, 'planned and hoped') to have a child in two years' time. But no human being ever makes that decision. It is God's alone to make.

So in this chapter we have seen that the birth and nurture of children is one very important way in which married couples serve God. In the next chapter we ask how the marriage relationship itself can serve God.

For study or discussion

1. What is God's purpose in giving the blessing of Genesis 1:28?

2. Think about attitudes to children. If you are preparing for marriage, be sure to talk about these questions.
    a. How do attitudes to children in our society differ from the Bible's attitude?

    b. Examine your own attitude. What makes you nervous or afraid at the prospect of having children? Commit these fears to God in prayer.

    c. Why do you want children? How do your reasons compare with God's reason? Pray that your reasons for wanting children will line up with God's reason.

3. How does the Bible link parenthood to serving God in his world?

4. Why is having children still important? Why not just focus on making more Christians?

5. What sort of people ought parents to be?

6. Think about teaching our children about the God who made the world.
   a. Why does it matter to teach our children the good news of Jesus?

   b. How and when can we do this, at different stages of their lives?

   c. What examples have you seen of good practice by parents you know?

   d. How practically can you do this better?

7. How will the teaching of this chapter affect how we educate our children?

8. Have you seen good role models of parents who have made personal or career sacrifices for the good of their children?

9. Why is it usually wrong deliberately not to have children?

10. How ought we to react if we, or others known to us, are unable to have children?

11. If you are preparing for marriage, what will your attitude be to contraception?

4 What is the point of sex and intimacy?

Melissa and Keith have been married for fifteen years now. They have three lovely children. They are both active in their local church in various ways, and seem the model Christian couple. Melissa is capable, attractive and energetic. Keith is fit and healthy, and a cheerful and popular leader in the church youth group.

What nobody knows is that their sex life has all but died. I guess Keith still wants it quite a bit, but the problem is that really Melissa doesn't any more. After all, they have had their children. She is tired and busy bringing them up. To be honest, sex doesn't really do anything much for her these days. She doesn't actually refuse Keith, but in various none-too-subtle ways she lets it be known that, although she would agree to it, really it is a bit of an unwelcome imposition.

And so Keith has all but given up. He tries to compensate by getting even more actively involved in the youth group and by keeping really busy at work. But when he is away on business trips it is increasingly hard not to seek some relief through internet pornography. To his dismay, he even found himself seriously considering following up one of the prostitute ads that he found in his hotel room.

Each of them in their different ways finds themselves asking, 'What is the point of trying to keep our sex life going in our marriage?'

In chapter 2 we saw that the whole of marriage is to be lovingly offered to God for his service. We saw that this may be divided into three broad areas, two positive and one negative. The negative one is the avoidance of sexual chaos, and we shall be looking at this in chapter 6. The positive ones are having children and the marriage relationship itself.

It is perhaps not too difficult to see how children might fit into God's purpose for looking after his world, as we have done in chapter 3. But what of the marriage relationship itself, the love of wife and husband for each other, expressed supremely in sexual intimacy and delight? What wider purpose can this possibly serve in God's world? Surely that must be classed as sex for the benefit of one another, rather than of God? Some may perhaps say that they can see how sex can work in the service of God when it leads to children, but not how sex and intimacy can serve God on other (i.e. most) occasions. And if sex serves God only when it leads to pregnancy, then most sex does not serve God! Such thinking would bring us right back to the suspicious and negative views of sex held by some of the early Church Fathers, such as Augustine, who reluctantly allowed it for the sake of children, but regarded it as essentially sinful apart from that.

The Bible does not share this negative attitude to sex. Sexual attractiveness, beauty, desire and delight are affirmed and accepted as a right and natural part of the world. In Psalm 45:11 we read of the king desiring the beauty of his bride, something which is affirmed as right and natural and a cause of rejoicing. In fact the Bible even speaks of God himself as feeling like that king, as a husband passionately desiring intimate delight with his wife. In Isaiah 62:5 we read that 'as the bridegroom rejoices over the bride, so shall your God rejoice over you.' This is bold imagery, possible only because the Bible is warmly in favour of sex within marriage.

Weddings are times for the glad voices of bridegroom and bride (e.g. Jeremiah 7:34), and when the best wine should be included on the menu (John 2:1–11). The wise man enjoys life with the wife he loves (Ecclesiastes 9:9). Isaac fondles Rebekah in a way that is entirely appropriate for her husband, but not for anyone else (Genesis 26:8). Jacob waits seven years for Rachel, and it seems like no time at all because he adores her (Genesis 29:20). Proverbs even tells the young married man unashamedly to have a great time with his young wife, letting her breasts satisfy his desires at all times (Proverbs 5:18–19). And of course the Song of Songs is full of unashamed erotic delight.

The question is, what is it about sex within marriage that is not only pleasurable but actually *good*, because it works in the service of God? Of course it can be pleasurable, but what good does it do? Or, in terms of our example at the beginning of the chapter, what is the *point* of Melissa and Keith taking urgent steps to rekindle their sexual intimacy and delight?

To build a good marriage, it is important to get sex into its proper place, which is neither too important nor too un-important, as we shall see.

Don't have too high a view of sex

First, we need to be aware that in our age, as in every age, there are voices clamouring for us to turn sex into a god or goddess. Gradually over the past century or so, the focus of thinking about sex and marriage has shifted away from children and towards the relationship itself.

The shift has not just been away from children; it has also been away from connection to wider family links. We focus on the 'nuclear family', and neglect belonging to a wider society. One influential sociologist has popularized the idea of what he calls 'pure relationships'. He does not mean what the Bible means by purity. He means relationships that are just one on one, untainted by ties or obligations to a wider family or society. These 'pure' relationships are held together only as long as both 'partners' think they are worth continuing. Sex is privatized and becomes just a personal lifestyle choice. All we need to think about, he implies, is you and me.

If we believe this, then relationship is all about you and me and our self-fulfilment. It really is 'sex in the service of us'. This is a far cry from the loving service of God in his world. What is more, if we think this way then it will not be long before we begin to think of sex as our saviour. After all, it is through sexual intimacy that I hope to achieve fulfilment and indeed true humanness. Through the self-fulfilment of sexual satisfaction I become the person I was meant to be. Through sex I discover myself. This, to some extent, is the conclusion of the movie *Titanic*, in which Rose (as an old lady) affirms that when, all those years ago, Jack became her lover he 'saved her'. From the time of the ancient Canaanites onwards it has been common to buy into this religion of sex as saviour. One (supposedly) Christian theologian even claims that sexual intercourse *is* communion with God. This is the worship of sex as god or goddess. But, since sex is not God, the Bible teaches that this kind of behaviour is the worship of idols. Therefore it always disappoints and leads to disillusion.

At the other extreme, however (and I want to spend more time on this), it is possible to have too low a view of sex. Sex within marriage is important. We are going to look at one Bible passage which spells out this importance, and then two further ways in which the Bible indicates or suggests how the marriage relationship may serve God in his world.

Don't have too low a view of sex

[1]Now concerning the matters about which you wrote: 'It is good for a man not to have sexual relations with a woman.' [2]But because of the temptation to sexual immorality, each man should have his own wife and each woman her own husband. [3]The husband should give to his wife her conjugal rights, and likewise the wife to her husband. [4]For the wife does not have authority over her own body, but the husband does. Likewise the husband does not have authority over his own body, but the wife does. [5]Do not deprive one another, except perhaps by agreement for a limited time, that you may devote yourselves to prayer; but then come together again, so that Satan may not tempt you because of your lack of self-control.

[6]Now as a concession, not a command, I say this.

(1 Corinthians 7:1–6)

At the start of 1 Corinthians 7 Paul begins to teach about questions the Corinthians had asked. Someone in Corinth had been saying (verse 1) 'It is good for a man not to have sexual relations with a woman.' (The NIV 'not to marry' is a mistranslation; the word is literally 'touch' and in these contexts always refers to sexual intimacy.) We deduce that these words are a quotation of someone else, because Paul immediately disagrees with them. Quite likely these were falsely spiritual people who were encouraging married couples to avoid sex, because sex was dirty or unspiritual.

There was a lot of sexual immorality in Corinth, as there is in our societies today. And therefore, says Paul in verse 2, it is much better to be married, if you can, and have regular sex within marriage. Wife and husband have equal 'conjugal rights' over each other: that is, the wife has the right to the husband's body in sex, and the husband to the wife's body. They owe it to each other to do all they can to satisfy each other's sexual desires.

Incidentally, we shy away from an expression like 'conjugal rights'. It sounds so cold. How can the exciting and spontaneous chemistry of sex simply be reduced to a matter of rights? And yet we all know that there are some lifestyle factors that can make an ongoing sexual relationship flourish, and others that can cause it to shrivel up and die. Some of these factors may lie outside our control, such as illness or poor living conditions. But many are within our control. For example, deliberately chosen overwork makes us less interested in sex. And pornography diverts sexual energies away from the one to whom we owe them. There are disciplines and rhythms of life that will cause sexual delight in marriage to flourish, and we ought to guard these lifestyles.

Indeed, if you are considering getting married, it is worth being aware that on your wedding day you surrender authority over your body to your wife or husband (verse 4). So you had better make sure you trust them. Paul is very concerned to prevent sex dying within marriages. So in verse 5 he tells them not to deprive one another of sex. The only exception that he reluctantly allows is if they both agree (and really agree, with no forcing on either side) to 'fast' from sex for a short time in order to give themselves in a special way to prayer. But even this must not be for too long, and is only allowed (verse 6) as a concession and not a command. It is often thought that the 'concession' of verse 6 is to allow some couples to marry. But this would make no sense of verse 2. Rather the 'concession' of verse 6 is to allow a couple a temporary 'fast' from sex (verse 5). Paul is in favour of sex within marriage and reluctantly allows a couple to suspend this for a limited time. The command is to keep the sexual relation flourishing insofar as it is within the couple's power.

The word translated 'devote' in verse 5 is a word that means giving time, energy and attention. If stopping sex means I can *devote* time, energy and attention to prayer, then the implication is that starting sex again means I will need to *devote* time, energy and attention to sex. This ought to be so obvious as not to need saying, but it is often neglected. Christians tend to focus on the epidemic of sexual activity outside marriage, but I suspect we ought to devote at least equal attention to the epidemic of sexual *in*activity within marriages. Before I was married, I understood that the Bible was against sex outside marriage. I was all too painfully aware of that red traffic light, much as I wished it was not there. In my mind, I suppose I was sitting at the lights in my bright red sports car waiting for the green light, at which point I imagined myself racing off into the sunset with a roaring libido for ever. I forgot that even the sportiest libido needs to be refuelled. It is important to remember not only that the Bible forbids sex outside marriage, but that it commends sex within marriage.

Many, if not most, couples will encounter problems in their sexual relationship at some stage of married life, and especially perhaps at the start. If this is you, please don't get unduly discouraged; you are in good company! Do not believe the absurdly unrealistic portrayals in the media of easily attained sexual paradise. The reality is that sex within marriage takes time. It needs to be worked at gently and patiently. You may need to ask for help; don't be in the least ashamed if you do. It is much better to seek out a discreet older Christian couple, or perhaps a doctor, for help, than to let the problems fester.

But it is important to work lovingly at this intimacy at the heart of marriage. Sometimes a newly married couple say to me that it feels a bit selfish to spend a good amount of relaxed time together, since this is what they want to do anyway! But it is not selfish. Because, by laying the foundations for a healthy intimacy and delight at the heart of marriage, they make it possible to grow a long-lived marriage where love will over-flow outwards to the blessing of many others in the years ahead. It may seem selfless to 'starve' time together in order to serve more outside the marriage, but in the longer term it is actually selfish, because the rest of us will have to pick up the pieces of a struggling or broken marriage. So, if you are engaged, so far as it is in your power, plan to have plenty of good relaxed time together especially in the first year, and after that, when, God willing, the foundations are laid, still guard those times together. Guard the fires at the heart so that the warmth of your love can spread outwards to others!

Having said this, we must remember that a happy sexual relationship in marriage will change its dynamics over time. After childbirth, special care will be needed for physical gentleness, and patience as well. And even in the absence of any illness or physical or psychological dysfunctions (which are all too common), a happily married couple in their eighties will express their delight differently from a couple in their twenties. There comes a time when, even for the most vigorous, 'desire [i.e. libido] fails' (Ecclesiastes 12:5). Even the strongly libidinous King David reached an age where nothing happened even when a very beautiful woman shared his bed (1 Kings 1:1–4). And yet intimacy and delight in each other can happily and contentedly survive the decay of physical desire.

At every age the principle remains, that in marriage each owes his or her body to the other, to give the other all the love and intimacy of which they are capable. There will be times when this is sheer delight on both sides. But there will be times when, for one of you, this will be more of a costly giving, when, for whatever reason, you have little or no desire for sex. At these times especially it is important to remember that on your wedding day you committed yourself sexually to your wife or husband for life. Make space for it as marriage goes on; nurture it and nourish it in love.

Sex at the heart of a relationship overflowing in loving service

But 1 Corinthians 7:1–6 on its own does not yet indicate how the marriage relationship itself can serve God. So we turn to two other Bible indicators of how this service of God works itself out. In each, the principle is that sexual intimacy and delight lie at the heart of a relationship in which the loving heart will overflow from that stable safe place out into loving service of others.

God's love for his bride Israel overflows in blessing for the world

The first Bible indicator is the theme of God the husband's love for Israel his bride (e.g. Hosea 1:2; Isaiah 54:5). We may call this God's marriage. He loves his people passionately and he calls on them to love him with an equally devoted and single-hearted love in return. It is an intense and passionate love, more passionate on God's side than any human marriage. The best and deepest sexual intimacy between a man and a woman is only a pale echo of the passionate devotion of God for his people.

Although it is a troubled marriage, broken again and again by the spiritual unfaithfulness of Israel, we must notice that even this passionate love relationship has an outward-looking focus. Right from the start, this intense love is meant to overflow into blessing for the world. Because of this covenant love, 'all the families of the earth shall be blessed' (Genesis 12:1–3). Just as Adam married Eve so that together they might care for the 'garden', so the Lord 'marries' Israel so that together they may properly rule and order his world. Israel was to be like a fruitful vine that takes root and fills the far corners of the world (Psalm 80:8–11). This is a picture of a marriage that overflows in blessing well beyond the borders of its own bedroom. If that was the purpose of God's marriage, how much more ought we to seek to serve him in our marriages. God wants our marriages to be echoes of his marriage. And this means that our marriages need a passionate heart of intimacy that overflows in blessing to others. This is the purpose of the marriage relationship.

Even in the Song of Songs, marriage overflows into fruitfulness

The second Bible example of marriage intimacy overflowing into wider usefulness is the Song of Songs. This may seem surprising, because many people think the Song of Songs is just about sexual desire and delight. This Bible book needs to be read on two levels at the same time. On one level it is a collection of love songs expressing beautifully and frankly the tensions and delights of a man and woman in love, reaching its high point in sexual union (Song 5:1). On another level, as a book in the Bible, it is natural and right to read it also as the love songs of the Lord, the God of the Bible, who is the bridegroom of his people, and their songs of answering love to him.

Both levels of reading are true. God loves his people like a man passionately in love with his wife, and his people respond in the same way to him. The unashamed delights of erotic love in marriage take their significance and wonder from the fact that they are a pale reflection of this greater and deeper love of God and his people.

The question is: does the Song of Songs indicate in any way that human sexual delight is used in the service of God? Many think it does not, and that the Song of Songs proves that God simply wants couples to have a wonderful time together, because that delight is a good thing – full stop. The Song, they say, is happily introspective, and so we may be in our marriages. And so, they say, the point of being married is simply to enjoy one another. Let's forget all this tough stuff about serving God. Let's get back to gazing into one another's eyes as we have wanted to do all the time. Forget the 'garden', and stay in the bedroom.

There are, however, two important indicators in these poems that sex really is to be used in the service of God. Both need some appreciation of poetry and poetic imagery.

The first indicator is the theme of spring flowers and autumn fruit. As with so many love songs, spring is in the air. For example, the bridegroom sings, 'Arise, my love, my beautiful one, and come away, for behold, the winter is past' (Song 2:10–11). In their love they visit the vineyards to see the grape blossom and the pomegranate flower (Song 7:12).

Love in the springtime is love in an atmosphere of beauty, fragrance, delight, and a world awash with possibilities and full of hope. But hope for what? The answer, in the language of the garden, is hope for the autumn. We forget that a garden in Bible cultures is not just a flower garden, producing flowers only for their beauty. It is an orchard and a vegetable garden, producing spring flowers in the hope that there will be autumn fruit and vegetables. It is a curiously modern reading that can imagine that the delight of springtime in these poems has nothing whatever to do with the hopes for fruit, or, to put it another way, that the sexual delight of this couple has nothing to do with hopes for building a home and family. So one liberal writer says of the Song, 'The intense delight which the lovers take in each other is clearly *an end in itself* which is not justified by further reference to having children, pleasing God, or anything else.' How wrong he is, and what a pedestrian and cardboard way to read the poems. They revel in the springtime of love because it gives hope for the autumn of fruitfulness. And fruitfulness is a great Bible picture, not only of children but more deeply of a world properly ordered and cultivated. As these lovers revel in their love, they grasp that this love overflows to play its part in caring for a needy world.

When you or I find ourselves 'falling in love' with our future wife or husband, we can now ask 'Why has God given me these feelings?' Why do I feel like a bird in springtime? The answer is, so that as a couple delighting in one another you can forge a new social unit whose heart is faithful love; and then out of that heart of faithful love can overflow generous love to others.

So the first indicator in the Song of Songs that marriage is outward-looking is the theme of spring flowers leading to autumn fruitfulness. The second indicator focuses on the identity of the bridegroom, the male lover. He is, in the poetic imagery, a kingly figure, a kind of image of the great King Solomon. Whether he is actually the historical Solomon, or whether this is a poetic device, doesn't matter. The point is that he is not just a handsome young man; he is a kingly figure. So, for example, when he appears in Song 3:6–11, he is surrounded by the mighty men of Israel. Whether literally or metaphorically, he is not only her lover but also Israel's king. He cannot gaze soft-focus into her eyes all the time. For he has a kingdom to rule and work to do. And presumably she must help him with this, as the royal princess does in Psalm 45. Their delight in one another is to overflow in usefulness and blessing to other people.

So, both in the theme of spring and autumn and in the theme of the king, these songs speak of a sexual delight that issues in fruitfulness to bring life to a needy world, and kingly rule to bring justice to a broken world. You may think it is a bit too grand or poetic to think of your marriage in these terms, but try! Consider how your faithful love for one another, fed and nourished through the delights of bodily intimacy, can overflow outwards to bring love and faithfulness to a needy world. Think about how, in partnership with one another, helping one another, your love can provide a centre of stable security; so that this safe home will become a refuge into which others can be welcomed. Think practically how in your marriage relationship your private intimacy can be at the heart of a relationship which overflows in love to others outside.

The principle is that faithful love cannot flow out from a marriage unless it is present as the heart of a marriage. As a good tree bears good fruit, so the usefulness of a marriage in bringing blessing to others depends on its inner secret of warm intimate love. This is nothing to do with success at sexual technique, as though only the couples who achieve the impossible athletic standards dangled before them in the lifestyle magazines can serve God! Nothing could be further from the truth (which is a relief for most of us, if we are honest!). For a couple who become obsessed with their 'success' or otherwise swiftly turn sex into an idol. It is precisely the couple who love *one another*, and not the experience of sex as such, who generate in their marriage an outflow of love to nourish a needy world.

Conclusion: putting sex in its proper place

We conclude that sex must be put in its proper place in marriage. On the one hand, it is not the be-all and end-all of marriage. Sex is not a god or goddess; sex cannot save us or give us our identity or fulfilment. But, on the other hand, sex is very important and the sexual relationship needs to be nurtured as the heart of a relationship of faithful love. Around sex there is friendship and companionship. And out of these flows hospitality, a home into which others can be welcomed, a family which serves and loves others in friendship and loves the unlovely. So we must nurture sex, but not as an end in itself. We nurture the private intimacy of marriage in order to keep the fires burning that will warm others outside. When sex is put in its proper place, neither too important nor neglected, then it will thrive as it was designed to flourish, as sex in the service of God.

For study or discussion

Read 1 Corinthians 7:1–6 and Song of Songs 4:1 – 5:1

1. What is the Bible's attitude to sex within marriage?

2. Think about contemporary attitudes to sex.
   a. How does our society encourage us to make a god of sex?

   b. Can you think of examples of this in movies, magazines or books?

   c. Where does this attitude lead?

3. Consider the sexual relationship within marriage.
   a. Why should a married couple keep their sexual relationship warm and alive?

   b. What kinds of things will stop this happening or make it difficult?

   c. Where would you turn for help if you have ongoing problems with the sexual relationship in your marriage?

4. Adam was clearly delighted with Eve in Genesis 2:23.
   a. Is there still delight in your marriage?

   b. If delight has grown dull, how can it be rekindled? What steps can you take to revitalize sex in your marriage?

5. Sex will not thrive where there is bad communication.
   a. How good are you at communicating your love for one another?

   b. How good are you at hearing your husband's or wife's love expressed to you? (And if you can't 'hear' it, what obstacles are preventing you?)

   c. Are there ways in which one of you 'knocks' the other (e.g. putting the other down in conversation or before friends)? How can you learn to affirm and praise your partner instead?

   d. How easy do you find it to share emotions, feelings, hurts?

   e. How good are you at listening to each other? (Remember Proverbs 18:13: 'If one gives an answer before he hears, it is his folly and his shame.')

   f. What is the area you find most difficult to talk about in marriage?

   g. How can you learn to communicate better?

6. Friendship is a very important part of a healthy marriage relationship.

   a. In what ways are you developing your friendship with one another?

   b. Do you have shared interests or activities?

   c. How is your friendship growing over time?

7. In what way is God's marriage in the Bible outward-looking?

8. In what ways is the marriage in the Song of Songs outward-looking?

9. Think about how your marriage will overflow into love for others.

   a. In what practical ways will safeguarding and nurturing the marriage relationship do good to others outside the marriage?

   b. Do you show hospitality? To whom, and why?

   c. What opportunities do you have for showing love to others outside your immediate family?

5 God's pattern for the marriage relationship

All through her childhood, marriage had seemed to Lydia a bit like war. Her father was a domineering man, a bully really. He used to speak unkindly to her mother, and rule the home in a quite scary way. When anything went wrong, it was never his fault. If he couldn't blame it on his wife, it must have been one of the children's fault. Lydia's mother was cowed into a rather pathetic shadowy existence. Lydia resolved she would never be like her.

When she went to her uncle and aunt, things were very different. Her aunt was a forceful career woman who really seemed to rule the roost. She made all the decisions and simply told her husband about it later. Although Lydia admired her aunt's spirit, she actually found herself feeling rather sorry for her uncle, or sometimes despising him. He did seem such a passive and downtrodden figure.

So when Lydia became a Christian and married Tony, she came away from the marriage preparation really puzzled. The evening had been all about 'headship' and 'submission', and she couldn't really make head or tail of it. I mean, she could see the words in the Bible. But she couldn't relate it to the dynamics of real life. And certainly it seemed to come from a different planet, so far as her background was concerned. But she wanted to learn. She could see that neither her parents nor her uncle and aunt made attractive role models for marriage, and she longed for something both workable and beautiful. But just what did the Bible mean by 'headship' and 'submission'?

In chapter 2 we saw that there are three purposes for marriage: children, relationship, and public order. And all of these are ways of serving the purposes of God. Chapters 3 and 4 explored the two positive ones: having children and then the marriage relationship. Before moving to the third purpose in chapter 6, we pause on the marriage relationship, to ask how this relationship is to work.

> [18]Three things are too wonderful for me;
>   four I do not understand:
> [19]the way of an eagle in the sky,
>   the way of a serpent on a rock,
> the way of a ship on the high seas,
>   and the way of a man with a virgin.
> (Proverbs 30:18–19)

When the wise man of Proverbs 30 looked around at the world he was filled with wonder. In this saying he selects three wonderful examples of things that make their way in difficult or puzzling places. He tells us these three as his warm-up for the fourth, which is his main point. He is filled with wonder as he watches an eagle make its way in the sky, a snake make its way over a rough rock, and a ship make its way over the turbulent seas. But these wonders are as nothing compared with the mystery of how a man makes his way in relations with a woman! This indeed is a mystery that is beyond his wisdom. For he knows that there is something about the opposite sex which is deeply mysterious. Many men and women have echoed his sense of wonder and mystery! And therefore we need the wisdom of the word of God to understand how we ought to relate as husband and wife. This is our subject now: the shape of marriage. Or, to put it another way, how ought husband and wife to relate to each other?

The Bible's answer is simple, politically incorrect, and deeply beautiful: the wife ought to submit to her husband as the church submits to Christ, and the husband ought to love his wife as Christ loves the church. We have referred more than once to the marriage of God to his people. This picture of God's marriage is the key to our subject.

To mention the 's' word (submission) would seem to be close to suicidal for a contemporary author. Some readers will want to close the book immediately. I want to encourage you to persevere, even if it makes you feel defensive or vulnerable. Misunderstood, this subject can cause great hurt and pain. But properly understood, I believe it leads to freedom and joy.

Even so, many Christians are defensive or apologetic about this teaching in the Bible. We are embarrassed that the Bible teaches wives to submit to their husbands. We fear that in some way it demeans women and rather wish that the Bible had put it in some other way. I was reading a book of marriage services for Christians from different denominations and noticed that the list of suggested Bible readings omitted the only three readings in the New Testament which are directly addressed to husbands and wives (Ephesians 5:22–33; Colossians 3:18–19; 1 Peter 3:1–7). This would have struck me as curious, except that all three Bible passages tell wives to submit to their husbands, and I am sure were omitted because the compilers simply could not stomach this teaching. When these passages are read in some churches, there are sniggers (if it is assumed we do not believe them any more), or a perceptible increase in tension (if it appears that some do still in fact believe them). So I am sure the compilers thought they were best ignored.

They were wrong. We need not be defensive. This is a beautiful pattern. It undermines equally the oppression of male chauvinism and the false dawn of aggressive secular feminism. We need to pay careful attention to this pattern. This is how God has made the world, with men and women made equally in his image, and entrusted equally with the joyful honour of governing his good world (Genesis 1:26–28). Equal, but different.

Nevertheless, as the story is told in Genesis 2, the man is created first (Genesis 2:7). The New Testament understands that this is of lasting significance (1 Timothy 2:13; 1 Corinthians 11:8), and therefore that men and women are equal but complementary. We need each other. We are not like the two halves of an hourglass, which may be exchanged for each other without anyone noticing the difference.

Indeed, we should expect that our bodily differences will be signs of deep differences. For we are not sexless spirits imprisoned in sexual bodies, but whole embodied people. And it is an irony that, while we rightly stress a holistic view of human beings in medicine, in other areas we are told to speak as if men and women are identical apart from a few minor anatomical and hormonal distinctives. On the contrary, our anatomical and hormonal distinctives point to whole persons who are male or female and therefore deeply and wonderfully different.

The problem in Genesis 3 is not just that Adam and Eve disobeyed God, but that the serpent turned God's proper order upside down. Adam ought to have been giving a loving lead, Eve ought to have submitted to that lead, and they ought both together to have ruled over the unruly serpent. Instead the serpent spoke to Eve, who listened to the serpent instead of to Adam, and Adam then listened to Eve (verse 17) instead of giving a godly lead. And it all ended in tears. This may be why in verse 16 God says to Eve, 'Your desire shall be for your husband.' This may well mean 'your desire will be to dominate your husband' (the same word is used in that sense in Genesis 4:7). God goes on, 'and he shall rule over you', which may mean 'rule over you as he ought to have done in the first place [lovingly]', or it may mean 'rule over you in an oppressive way never intended by God'.

Either way, relations between men and women have been badly soured by human disobedience to God. Since then, both men and women have behaved badly towards one another. This distorted relationship is beautifully restored in God's pattern for marriage. Men and women, who share equally in salvation in Christ (Galatians 3:28), now learn as equals to relate as they ought to have related since the creation of the world.

The three passages we need to consider (Ephesians 5:22–33; Colossians 3:18–19; 1 Peter 3:1–7) come in collections of teaching about how different people (masters and servants, parents and children, citizens and rulers, husbands and wives) ought to relate to one another (Ephesians 5:22 – 6:9; Colossians 3:18 – 4:1; 1 Peter 2:13 – 3:7).

Some of the instructions are given so that Christians will not scandalize their society and bring upon themselves needless persecution. That is, some of the commands to submit are given not because this submission will always be necessary, but because it was the custom in their culture, and if they had not submitted it would have caused a scandal. This is particularly true of teaching for slaves; at no point does the New Testament give a reason why the institution of slavery ought to continue. But it is different for marriage, as we shall see from the Bible passages we are about to consider.

Wives are not told to submit to their husbands just because it happens to be the custom of the day. Instead, the apostles give 'God reasons' for them to do this. There are two of these 'God reasons'. The first is that submission is how God the Son relates to God the Father in the Trinity. 'But I want you to understand that the head of every man is Christ, the head of a wife is her husband, and the head of Christ is God' (1 Corinthians 11:3). This submission is reinforced in 1 Corinthians 15:24, where Paul says that at the very end of time Jesus 'delivers the kingdom to God the Father'. And it is supported by Jesus' own testimony that in his earthly life 'I do nothing on my own authority' (John 8:28).

The second 'God reason' is that the shape of human marriage is to follow the same shape as God's marriage to his people, which is the shape of Christ's marriage to his church (Ephesians 5:22–33). Because these are 'God reasons', we need to understand that this is the pattern for every age and all cultures. This is God's shape for marriage and we need to understand it.

The shape of marriage in Ephesians 5:22–33 and Colossians 3:18–19

22Wives, submit to your own husbands, as to the Lord. 23For the husband is the head of the wife even as Christ is the head of the church, his body, and is himself its Saviour. 24Now as the church submits to Christ, so also wives should submit in everything to their husbands.

25Husbands, love your wives, as Christ loved the church and gave himself up for her, 26that he might sanctify her, having cleansed her by the washing of water with the word, 27so that he might present the church to himself in splendour, without spot or wrinkle or any such thing, that she might be holy and without blemish. 28In the same way husbands should love their wives as their own bodies. He who loves his wife loves himself. 29For no one ever hated his own flesh, but nourishes and cherishes it, just as Christ does the church, 30because we are members of his body. 31'Therefore a man shall leave his father and mother and hold fast to his wife, and the two shall become one flesh.' 32This mystery is profound, and I am saying that it refers to Christ and the church. 33However, let each one of you

love his wife as himself, and let the wife see that she respects
her husband.
(Ephesians 5:22–33)

[18]Wives, submit to your husbands, as is fitting in the Lord.
[19]Husbands, love your wives, and do not be harsh with them.
(Colossians 3:18–19)

Just before this passage in Paul's letter to the Ephesians, he
writes (verse 21) 'submitting to one another out of reverence
for Christ'. It is a mistake to think he is telling each Christian to
submit to every other Christian, since he goes on to give
asymmetrical commands. He does not tell husbands to submit
to their wives, parents to their children, or masters to their
slaves. He means, 'Submit to one another in all the contexts
in which submission is appropriate: that is, the contexts I am
about to explain to you.'

He begins (verses 22–24) by telling the wives to submit to
their husbands as to the Lord (Jesus). Submission is widely
misunderstood. People think it means the woman has to be a
cowering servant, to be seen but not heard, scurrying around
doing everything she is told, always being forced to pick up the
worst jobs in the home, and certainly not being allowed to
work outside the home.

But Christian submission is not like this at all. To submit is
not a passive thing; it does not mean to be made subject or
forced into subjection. To submit is something all Christians
are called to do actively and voluntarily in appropriate contexts.
As citizens they are to submit to the civil authorities (Romans
13:1–7); as church members they are to submit to their church
leaders (Hebrews 13:17; 1 Peter 5:5); as children they are to
submit to their parents (Ephesians 6:1; Colossians 3:20; compare
the example of the Lord Jesus in Luke 2:51); if slaves, they are
to submit to their masters (Titus 2:9; 1 Peter 2:18; compare
'obey' in Ephesians 6:5 and Colossians 3:22); and if wives, they

are to submit to their husbands (Ephesians 5:22; Colossians 3:18; 1 Peter 3:1).

So all Christians are called upon to submit in appropriate circumstances, and most Christians are called upon to exercise authority in other circumstances. For example, a wife submits to her husband while her children submit to her. A husband submits to his pastor while his wife submits to him. Exercising authority does not increase my status or value, any more than submitting to authority reduces my status or value. For example, if I cease to be a pastor, my value in God's sight does not diminish because now, instead of church members submitting to me, I must submit to my pastors. It is absurd to think that submission is demeaning to me as a person. On the contrary, every day I am called actively and deliberately to submit to those to whom God calls me to submit.

These submissions differ from one another. A child submits to parents in one way. A citizen submits to the civil authorities in another way. And a wife submits to her husband in a different way again. But all these submissions are voluntary and honourable things to do. After all, even Christ himself submits voluntarily to the Father (1 Corinthians 15:24–28). The Christian submits to those in authority over him or her as an expression of his or her submission to God, and in recognition that God has put order into society, for our good and to protect us from chaos. Incidentally, to 'submit' means something very similar to 'obey'; we see this most clearly in 1 Peter 3:4–5, where Peter says that godly women *submitted* to their husbands following the model of Sarah, who *obeyed* Abraham. That is, their submission is modelled on Sarah's obedience. But we must remember that there are always limits to submission and obedience, in that we must always obey God rather than people if the two obediences come into conflict (e.g. Acts 4:19–20).

The flip side of submission in a relationship is headship. Christ is the head of his body, the church (Colossians 1:18;

2:18–19; Ephesians 1:22–23; 4:15–16). And, in a different way, he is the head of every authority on earth (Colossians 2:9–10). But the difference is that the church submits willingly and joyfully to Christ, whereas rebellious powers do not submit to him until in the end they are forced to. The wife's submission in marriage is to be a voluntary and joyful submission, not an enforced one. She submits to her husband as the church submits lovingly to Christ, not as rebellious powers in the universe submit reluctantly to Christ. Nowhere is the husband told to make sure his wife submits, and only tyrannical husbands will try. Neither Paul nor Peter writes: 'Husbands, make sure your wives submit.' If, as a husband, I were to try to make my wife submit, her proper response would be: 'Mind your own business! *Your* calling is to serve and to love me. My submission is my free response to the God who loves me. It is up to me to submit, not up to you to make me submit!' So the submission of the wife in marriage is to be a glad and willing submission.

But the really significant thing about the Ephesians passage is not that wives are to submit. After all, that on its own would have caused no surprise to Paul's contemporaries. The real surprise is the much longer and more challenging command to husbands. For if women behave badly, men behave badly at least as much, and seem here to need nearly three times the correction. In the original Greek, Paul writes 40 words to the wives about submission, but 115 words to the husbands about sacrificial love. How is the husband to behave? The male chauvinist may have been cheering verses 22–24, in which the wives are told to submit: now at last she will treat me as I deserve, he thinks, waiting on me hand and foot and generally being subservient to make my life easier. Not a bit. The model for the husband is the way Christ treats his church, which is to give himself up even to death for her. Not only is he not to be harsh with her (Colossians 3:19), a peculiarly male tendency; on the contrary, he is to love her whatever it costs him. The shape of marriage for the husband is the shape of the cross.

C. S. Lewis writes that 'the headship' of the husband is not expressed in husbands doing what they like, but 'in him whose marriage is most like a crucifixion; whose wife receives most and gives least' and is 'least lovable'. The crown given to the husband is a crown of thorns. Lewis says that the real danger is not that husbands will grasp this crown too eagerly, but that they will let their wives wear it. He is right. The main challenge of this great passage in Ephesians is to husbands. We who are husbands need sufficient guts to be beauticians: that is, to give ourselves in loving serving leadership of our wives, so that through our love they become even more beautiful inside (Ephesians 5:27).

It is very important to hold on to this beautiful pattern. For what feminists fail to realize is that if we jettison verses 22–24, about submission, we must also jettison 25–33, about sacrificial love.

The shape of marriage in 1 Peter 3:1–7

[1]Likewise, wives, be subject to your own husbands, so that even if some do not obey the word, they may be won without a word by the conduct of their wives – [2]when they see your respectful and pure conduct. [3]Do not let your adorning be external – the braiding of hair, the wearing of gold, or the putting on of clothing – [4]but let your adorning be the hidden person of the heart with the imperishable beauty of a gentle and quiet spirit, which in God's sight is very precious. [5]For this is how the holy women who hoped in God used to adorn themselves, by submitting to their husbands, [6]as Sarah obeyed Abraham, calling him lord. And you are her children, if you do good and do not fear anything that is frightening.

[7]Likewise, husbands, live with your wives in an understanding way, showing honour to the woman as the

weaker vessel, since they are heirs with you of the grace of life, so that your prayers may not be hindered.
(1 Peter 3:1–7)

One very practical question is this: ought I to continue playing my part in this pattern if my spouse refuses to play his or hers?

The answer for the man has been given in Ephesians 5. Christ did not love the church because the church first submitted in loving obedience. He loved her first, and through his love drew her to himself with cords of love. In the same way, the husband is called to love his wife sacrificially whether or not she gladly plays her part with a happy submission.

But what of the wife? We need to know what to say to the wife whose husband really isn't very Christlike. Ought she or ought she not still to submit to him, imperfect as he is? Some wives will want to say, 'This pattern is well and good, even beautiful, if – and only if – the men behave better than they actually do. When and if my husband behaves remotely like Christ then I will gladly submit.'

Peter's teaching is a bracing challenge to this, as it is to other Christian submissions. Peter is particularly concerned for Christians being badly treated. He speaks to slaves with unjust masters (1 Peter 2:18), and now to wives with unbelieving husbands (1 Peter 3:1). Even these badly treated wives are in principle to submit, out of reverence for Christ. Indeed, they are to follow Sarah's example of not only submitting but obeying, so that by the precious jewel of a gentle and quiet spirit they may, God willing, win their husbands to Christ. And so we see that it is not only the husband's part in marriage which is shaped by the cross. For the wife too is to submit even to unfair treatment, just as Christ himself suffered unjust treatment on the cross (1 Peter 2:21–23). Both the husband, in his cross-shaped love, and the wife, in her cross-shaped submission, are to follow in the footsteps of Jesus Christ.

Having said this, we must remember that this general teaching may need to be qualified in cases of domestic abuse. When a husband abuses his wife physically or sexually in the home, there are issues of justice which come into play. He has no right to do this. Society at large is right to legislate against it, and the police are right to do all they can to stamp it out. However willing a godly wife is to submit under difficult circumstances, the rest of us may have to step in to protect her from abusive behaviour.

And again, as in Ephesians 5, the command to the husbands (if they are listening) in 1 Peter 3:7 is bracing. They are to 'live with' their wives 'in an understanding way, showing honour to the woman as the weaker vessel'. We who are husbands need to learn to understand our wives, the physical and psychological rhythms of their bodies, what they go through in childbirth, in breast-feeding, in all the stages of motherhood, when the children fly the nest, in the menopause, and in old age. We are to live with them according to understanding, recognizing that in some respects (and only some!) they are weaker than us. They are not weaker in intellect (far from it), nor in wisdom (after all, the woman in verses 1–6 is a believer married to an unbeliever, so Peter would clearly regard her as wiser than her husband!), nor in bravery in the face of pain (particularly in childbirth). But on average, in pure physical terms, women are not as strong. Even in our politically correct era they compete separately in the Olympics. And therefore in this respect we who are husbands are to care for them and not expect them simply to be replicates of ourselves (thank God).

We are to do this because, in a Christian marriage, they are heirs with us of the grace of life (that is, eternal life), equal in dignity and destiny in Christ. And we are to do this because otherwise our prayers will be hindered (verse 7). It is not clear whether this is our prayers as men, or our joint prayers as couples. But for either to be hindered is very serious. If I am inconsiderate to my wife, I cannot expect God to listen to my prayers. God will stop listening to my prayers, and penalties don't come a lot more serious than that.

How does God's shape for marriage become distorted?

When we ask what this pattern means in practice, it is help-ful first to see four ways in which the pattern can be spoiled. Two come from men behaving badly and two from women behaving badly.

The tyrannical husband

First, the pattern is spoiled by the tyrannical husband. He is domineering, exploitative, oppressive, bossy and selfish. He throws his weight around in the home, expects his wife to do what he wants, and expects his life to be made easier while his wife pays the price. It is all too easy for a tired or short-tempered husband to justify his roughness by saying he is 'giving a strong lead'. But tyranny is horrible, and Christlike headship ought to be the complete opposite to this.

The bossy wife

Second, the pattern is spoiled by the bossy wife who wants, like Eve in the garden, to take the lead, to exercise her own autonomy as the mistress of her fate and the captain of her soul. Far from a gentle and quiet spirit, this wife insists on inter-changeability of role in every way, and the result is likely to be war in the home. There is something deeply unattractive about the bossy wife.

The mousy wife

Third – and this may come as a surprise – the pattern is spoiled by the wife who behaves as a doormat. Perhaps her husband is a bit of a tyrant, and she decides simply to cooperate, to knuckle under. She is pliable and biddable and does just what he wants.

In so doing she abdicates the dignity of working alongside him in a noble partnership in the 'garden'. She places herself on the level of the animals, becoming what someone has called 'his pliable kitten': a kind of toy girl with whom he plays, but who has lost her dignity.

Instead, she ought to be using her wisdom to be his fellow-worker in the 'garden'. He ought to be so grateful to have such a hard-working, wise and generous wife alongside him. Like the fine wife of Proverbs 31:10–31 (who is 'wisdom' personified), or David's future wife Abigail trying to save everyone from disaster (1 Samuel 25), or Priscilla with Aquila (Acts 18:26; Romans 16:3–4), she ought to be a source of wise counsel and a valued partner.

We may ask how this active partner-wife can at the same time show Christian submission even to a less-than-Christlike husband. It is a difficult line to walk, to be an active partner without slipping into becoming domineering. But it is important for a wife not to let her idea of submission make her surrender her great dignity as the man's equal partner in serving God.

The abdicator husband

But fourth, and in my view most significantly of all, the pattern is spoiled when the husband abdicates his responsibilities, as Adam does in Genesis 3. I suspect that most of us husbands need to repent of this. The calling to cross-shaped leadership is just too costly, and we look for decent ways to avoid it, whether by needlessly long hours at the office or by excessive time at the sports club, abdicating our responsibilities as caring husbands and good fathers.

What does God's pattern look like in practice?

I am often asked to be more specific and practical in defining what headship and submission mean in practice. I am very reluctant to do this, because there are as many ways in which this pattern is worked out in practice as there are Christian couples. It would be terribly easy to lay down a system of rules, which would perhaps look outwardly as if they conformed to God's pattern when in fact they had lost the heart of it. Because this pattern is at heart a matter of attitudes, not rules.

At the heart of this pattern is the husband who consciously reminds himself again and again that he is called to be like Christ going to the cross in his marriage: to lead by serving and loving and caring whatever the cost to himself. At every stage of married life he does a kind of crucifixion audit on the way he is behaving. That is, he measures up the way he actually treats his wife against the way Christ treated the church when he went to the cross for her. And when he does that, again and again he repents and seeks God's grace to become ever so slightly more like Christ.

And at the heart of this pattern also is the wife who consciously reminds herself that she is to cultivate the gentle and quiet spirit of dignified honourable submission, serving alongside her husband with equal dignity, using her gifts to the full, but nevertheless encouraging him to take his place of Christlike headship in their marriage. She deliberately adopts this beautiful attitude in rebellion against all that society tells her to be. And she adopts it in spite of her husband's faults, and knowing that it will sometimes cost her to do it. She will not do it because her church expects it of her, or because her husband forces her, but because she loves God and longs to do his will.

What is the impact of God's pattern on the world?

God's pattern or shape for marriage knocks spots off every other pattern invented by humankind, from the oppression of the chauvinist to the competitive 'equality' of the feminist. But it is a delicate pattern, which works the better the more Christlike the husband is in his sacrificial love, and the more Christlike the wife is in her sacrificial submission. However, delicate though it is, all couples ought to make it their aim repeatedly to set and reset their relational compasses by it.

It is God's shape. And when it is approximated, the impact on the watching world can be considerable. Some years ago I read of a dispute in Britain between the Foreign Office and the Treasury. The argument was about which British Ambassadors would be provided with a Rolls Royce for their official duties in a foreign capital. The Treasury unsurprisingly wanted these wonderful cars restricted to a few: perhaps Washington, Moscow and Paris. The Foreign Office argued for many more, and I love their reasoning. Most people in a foreign capital have never been to Britain, they said. But when they see this magnificent car gliding through their streets with the Union flag on the bonnet, they will say to themselves, 'I have not been to Britain. I don't know much about Britain. But if they make cars like that there [and in those days we did!], then Britain must be a wonderful place.'

In a similar way, I like to think that men and women may say to themselves as they watch a Christian marriage: 'I have never seen God. Sometimes I wonder, when I look at the world, if God is good, or if there is a God. But if he can make a man and woman love one another like this; if he can make this husband show costly faithfulness through sickness as well as health; if he can give him resources to love when frankly there is nothing in it for him; well, then he must be a good God. And if he can give this wife grace to submit so beautifully, with such an attractive gentle spirit under terrible trials, then again he must be a good God.' If you are married or preparing for marriage, pray that others may be able to say this of you in the years ahead.

For study or discussion

Read Genesis 3:1–24, Ephesians 5:22–33, Colossians 3:18–19 and 1 Peter 3:1–7.

1. Why do we feel defensive about saying that wives should submit to their husbands?

2. How does our society misunderstand this teaching?

3. How do we know that this teaching still applies today?

4. In terms of the relationship between Adam and Eve, what went wrong in the garden of Eden?

5. For wives. Think about Christian submission.
   a. In what other contexts are Christians to submit?

   b. What does Christian submission mean (and not mean)? Think particularly about how you can show respect to your husband, even when you think he is wrong.

   c. What will Christian submission mean in your marriage?

6. For husbands. Think about Christlike headship.
   a. What is the husband told to do in marriage, and why?

b. In what ways is your wife 'weaker' and how will you love her especially in these areas?

c. In what practical ways can you love your wife sacrificially, at home, in parenting, in sharing of chores, etc?

7. In what ways are both husbands and wives to follow the example of the cross?

8. In what four ways can God's pattern be spoiled?

9. If you are married, test your marriage against these four distortions and God's perfect pattern. What practical steps can you take to move in the right direction?

6 What is the point of the marriage institution?

Why not just live together anyway?

> Martin had just announced his engagement, and was being congratulated at coffee time at work. He and Kathy were Christians. But although his colleagues seemed pleased, he knew that about two-thirds of them were already living quite openly with their boyfriends or girlfriends. And, to be honest, although they tried to be pleased for Martin, they couldn't really understand why he was bothering with marriage.
>
> One of them, Max, had been quite involved with his Christian Union at school and knew quite a bit about the Bible and Christian faith. Max challenged Martin (in a not unfriendly way): 'We're all pleased for you, of course. But why *don't* you and Kathy just live together? It'd be much cheaper and it's much more sensible really – much less trouble if it doesn't work out. Or (with a hint of hostility) I suppose you think the rest of us are "living in sin", do you?'

It was Groucho Marx, in the film *Animal Crackers*, who said that 'marriage is a great institution, but who wants to live in an institution?' A good friend of mine even proposed to his wife by asking her, with a twinkle in his eye, if she wanted to join him by coming to live in an institution! My friend was right. Marriage is a great institution. It is one of the great 'givens' of the world, both in the sense that it is not negotiable (because it is given in creation) and in the sense that it is a gift of God's grace. In this chapter we explore from the Bible why it is good, and why the boundaries and shape of marriage are a blessing. We ask, 'What is the point of the marriage institution?'

In chapter 2 we saw that there are three purposes for marriage: children, relationship, and public order. And each of these is to be used in the service of God. Chapter 3 explored the purpose of children and chapters 4 and 5 the purpose and shape of the marriage relationship. We turn now to public order: marriage as a safeguard against sexual chaos.

Sex is to be surrounded by the marriage boundary

Many people think that boundaries are not good, just annoyingly restrictive and arbitrary. The boundaries are clear: the Bible teaches consistently that sexual intimacy is good within marriage and wrong in all other contexts. In both the Old and New Testaments there are two distinct word groups. On the one hand, there are words for 'adultery' or 'to commit adultery'. Adultery is when a married person has sex with someone who is not their husband or wife.

The other group is usually translated 'sexual immorality', or, in the older versions, 'fornication'. In Greek this is the word group from which we get 'pornography' (which means the portrayal of sexually immoral behaviour). Sexual immorality has a broader meaning than adultery. It covers all sexual intimacy outside of marriage, including sex before marriage, sex while living together, homosexual acts, and sex with animals.

> Let marriage be held in honour among all, and let the marriage
> bed be undefiled, for God will judge the sexually immoral and
> adulterous.
> (Hebrews 13:4)

The Bible speaks consistently against this because it understands the goodness of marriage. The boundaries of marriage
need to be guarded. This is what the writer to the Hebrew
Christians means when he writes, 'Let marriage be held in
honour among all, and let the marriage bed be undefiled, for
God will judge the sexually immoral [the *pornos*: anyone who
indulges in sexual intimacy outside marriage] and adulterer'
(Hebrews 13:4). Adultery obviously dishonours marriage; but
so does all sexual immorality. Marriage is to be held in honour
as the only right context for sex. The Bible is clear on this.

This means that to love another person enough for sex means
to love them enough to have publicly committed yourself to
them for life in marriage. Short of that commitment, however
passionately you may say you love them, actually you don't love
them nearly enough for sex. So the proper Christian response to
a couple who want to sleep together unmarried is to ask: 'How
much do you love one another? Do you really love one another
enough for sex? For if you really do, then you will show that love
by *first* making the public commitment of marriage. And if you
are not ready for that public promise, then you are not ready for
sex, however much you may want it and feel that you love one
another. It isn't simply a question of what or how you feel,
because love is much more than feelings, and feelings alone are a
very unreliable guide to love.'

Human beings rebel against this boundary

Human beings have always kicked against this institution and
resented these clear boundaries. This includes people like me

who write about these things. We all fall short, in thought and desire if not in deed. Let those who think they stand take heed lest they fall.

In the last half-century living together unmarried is easily the most significant way that God's boundary has been crossed. This custom began in a small way in the 1960s amongst divorcees, but is now most common among young couples who have never married. Around the turn of the millennium about 40% of British women in their late twenties were living unmarried with a man, and presumably a similar proportion of men were living unmarried with a woman. As this custom works its way up the age groups, the government estimates that between about 1996 and 2021 the proportion of all couples who live together unmarried will roughly double, from 12% to about 22%.

Some of these cohabitations lead on to marriage, but many more break up and are followed by subsequent cohabitations with other partners. A large and detailed statistical study showed that two-thirds of those getting married between 1985 and 1992 had lived with at least one partner before marriage (sometimes but not always including their eventual marriage partner). In history there have been many different cultural ways to enter marriage. These have at times included what has been called 'common-law marriage', in which a man and woman living together were regarded by their society as being married. But what we see now is different. Couples choose to live together in a relationship which is *by definition* not marriage; marriage is available to them, but they choose not to enter it. This is not at all like the old 'common-law marriage'.

In this chapter I want to help us to understand why, paradoxically, this loosening of God's boundaries is a move towards slavery and away from freedom, towards law and away from grace. That is, I want us to see what is the point of the marriage institution and why its boundaries are gifts of God's grace. If you are living together unmarried or thinking of doing so, I do not want to condemn you, but to help you see that you are choosing a fragile alternative. I want to invite you into God's good gift of marriage. If you are a Christian, I want to help you see how we can commend marriage, not as restrictive 'do-gooders', but with cheerfulness and confidence.

God has put moral order into creation

First, I need to say a word about the created order. This is a counter-cultural idea, but it is very important. The Bible teaches that God made the universe. Never mind the debates about exactly how or when; they will be distractions from our subject. But God the Creator made the universe; it all comes from his hand. And he made it an ordered place. As the story is told in the structured form of Genesis 1, we see boundaries being put in place: between sky and earth, between waters and waters, and so on. There would be no point in doing science if there were no order in the universe. Scientists do not create order, they discover it.

But the order in the universe is not just in physical things. It is moral and not just material. There is also order in moral things and in how human beings relate. Just as a scientist does not invent physical order, but discovers it, so we do not invent morality, but rather discover in the Bible the morality that has been given to us by a good God.

To say this about sex goes right against the grain with many people today, who think that our 'sexuality' is some fluid substance that can be shaped by us any way we choose. There is no order given by God, they say, only rules made by power-hungry human groups wanting to impose their way on others. So 'the church' is seen as a group of traditionalist human beings who just want to impose their morality on the rest, who strongly resent this unwanted intrusion into their personal freedom.

It is important, therefore, to make it clear that we do not want to impose anything on anybody, but rather to say, 'This is how the world *is*; and we ignore it at our peril.' This includes sex. God has so constructed us that sex is safe and fruitful in marriage, but dangerous and destructive outside. This is how the world is. We can cut across that order if we choose. I can cut across the ordered rule of gravity by jumping out of a high window if I choose. But I cannot cut across the created order without harming myself and probably others. In the area of sex, we see plenty of evidence of that harm in our society as we are engulfed in sexual chaos. The ordered boundaries of marriage are given for our good.

The Bible chooses at least two ways to illustrate the disaster of sex outside marriage. Both are vividly argued in the book of Proverbs. These passages are addressed particularly to a young man; but it is easy enough to take the principles and apply them to women and men of all ages.

Sex outside marriage is disastrous

It leads to costly waste of energy

¹My son, be attentive to my wisdom;
  incline your ear to my understanding,
²that you may keep discretion,
  and your lips may guard knowledge.
³For the lips of a forbidden woman drip honey,
  and her speech is smoother than oil,
⁴but in the end she is bitter as wormwood,
  sharp as a two-edged sword.
⁵Her feet go down to death;
  her steps follow the path to Sheol;
⁶she does not ponder the path of life;
  her ways wander, and she does not know it.

[7]And now, O sons, listen to me,
   and do not depart from the words of my mouth.
[8]Keep your way far from her,
   and do not go near the door of her house,
[9]lest you give your honour to others
   and your years to the merciless,
[10]lest strangers take their fill of your strength,
   and your labours go to the house of a foreigner,
[11]and at the end of your life you groan,
   when your flesh and body are consumed,
[12]and you say, 'How I hated discipline,
   and my heart despised reproof!
[13]I did not listen to the voice of my teachers
   or incline my ear to my instructors.
[14]I am at the brink of utter ruin
   in the assembled congregation.'

[15]Drink water from your own cistern,
   flowing water from your own well.
[16]Should your springs be scattered abroad,
   streams of water in the streets?
[17]Let them be for yourself alone,
   and not for strangers with you.
[18]Let your fountain be blessed,
   and rejoice in the wife of your youth,
   [19]a lovely deer, a graceful doe.
Let her breasts fill you at all times with delight;
   be intoxicated always in her love.
[20]Why should you be intoxicated, my son,
      with a forbidden woman
   and embrace the bosom of an adulteress?
[21]For a man's ways are before the eyes of the LORD,
   and he ponders all his paths.
[22]The iniquities of the wicked ensnare him,
   and he is held fast in the cords of his sin.

> [23] He dies for lack of discipline,
> and because of his great folly he is led astray.
>
> (Proverbs 5:1–23)

In this passage the 'son' (verse 1) of the teacher or father is warned to keep clear of the 'forbidden woman' (3). This means the woman who is outside the structure and security of family life, the 'loose woman' who is happy to have sex outside the boundary of marriage. In a similar way we should warn a young woman against the 'loose' young man who wants to sleep with her without giving her the protection of marriage.

But notice the reason given, which is not simply 'it is wrong' (although it is). The reason is that if you go outside the boundaries of marriage for sex, you will 'give your honour' (that is, your substance, your wealth) to others (9), and the fruit of your strength and energy will be wasted instead of being used to build up a stable and fruitful family (10).

In our society we see this in the bitter fruit of sexual chaos, in the burden of maintenance payments after divorce, in the personal and social cost of the increasing numbers living on their own, in the mushrooming statistics for sexually transmitted diseases and HIV/AIDS, and in the sadness of old age carrying the scars of broken relationships. It may be fun at the time, but in the end you will be sad that you didn't care about God's boundaries (11–14). Instead, God's general plan is that we use our sexual energies in loving faithfulness to wife or husband, to build a stable and fruitful home (15–19). That is, use your sex in the service of God.

It leads to destructive jealousies

> [20] My son, keep your father's commandment,
> and forsake not your mother's teaching.
> [21] Bind them on your heart always;
> tie them around your neck.

22When you walk, they will lead you;
 when you lie down, they will watch over you;
 and when you awake, they will talk with you.
23For the commandment is a lamp and the teaching a light,
 and the reproofs of discipline are the way of life,
24to preserve you from the evil woman,
 from the smooth tongue of the adulteress.
25Do not desire her beauty in your heart,
 and do not let her capture you with her eyelashes;
26for the price of a prostitute is only a loaf of bread,
 but a married woman hunts down a precious life.
27Can a man carry fire next to his chest
 and his clothes not be burned?
28Or can one walk on hot coals
 and his feet not be scorched?
29So is he who goes in to his neighbour's wife;
 none who touches her will go unpunished.
30People do not despise a thief if he steals
 to satisfy his appetite when he is hungry,
31but if he is caught, he will pay sevenfold;
 he will give all the goods of his house.
32He who commits adultery lacks sense;
 he who does it destroys himself.
33Wounds and dishonour will he get,
 and his disgrace will not be wiped away.
34For jealousy makes a man furious,
 and he will not spare when he takes revenge.
35He will accept no compensation;
 he will refuse though you multiply gifts.
 (Proverbs 6:20–35)

In this passage the young man is warned against crossing the boundaries because it is like lighting a fire next to his chest; he will be burned (verse 27). Or like walking on hot coals; you can't do it without being scorched (28). The reason is that outside the boundaries of marriage, sex stirs up incredibly strong jealousies. Human beings are hard-wired to want 100% sexual loyalty from their man or woman, and bitterly to resent any intrusion into this loyalty. We will forgive a thief if he repays his theft, but nothing can compensate for the theft of the sexual loyalty of the man or woman pledged to me in loyalty (29–35).

When the marriage boundaries are crossed by any kind of sex outside marriage, the jealousies that are rightly stirred up lead to hatred and violence (if they are expressed) or to misery and depression (if they are internalized). Crossing the boundaries is not a recipe for a free and happy society; rather it leads to misery and violence. Self-serving sex is self-destructive sex. For these reasons marriage needs to be held in honour.

Marriage is given to us; we do not invent it

Marriage is a God-given institution, given graciously as part of the created order (Genesis 2:24). This is a blessing. The alternative would be that each couple would have to invent the terms of their own relationship, which is a recipe for insecurity and uncertainty. Happily, we do not have to invent marriage because it has been invented for us.

This ought to be a great relief. For the alternative would be that each couple would have to construct its own chosen kind of relationship, hoping against hope that what had been put together would work.

When a man and a woman prepare for marriage, a thousand and one things have to be negotiated. They have to negotiate with both families and each other about the wedding ceremony and party. They have to decide where to live, what jobs to do, how to furnish their home, what friendships to develop, and so on.

But the one thing they do not have to negotiate is marriage

itself. They do not have to get in the lawyers to agree whether or not they are free to sleep with others, how long the marriage should last, whether it should be secret or public, and so on.

Of course they can negotiate all these things and enter into a contract agreed between them on their terms, but, if they do, they are not getting *married*, but entering some humanly constructed contract that masquerades as marriage. To invent the terms of the relationship fills the whole adventure with fear and insecurity.

The day we get married we enter the institution of marriage

And on the day they get married, they enter this institution. They do not gradually grow into it. People speak a lot about the quality of a couple's relationship. Some people speak of marriage as an ideal to be sought. So, they say, we strive to build the quality of our relationship towards the marriage ideal, while recognizing that we will always fall short. If we think like this, then we replace the institution by a process. We might mischievously imagine a couple reporting in a Christmas letter, 'We've had a good year together, and feel we are significantly *more married* this year than last, probably up to about 87% now,' or, 'It's not been such a good year and we feel rather less married now; we feel maybe we've slipped to perhaps 63%.'

This is what happens when people say that 'marriage is just a piece of paper'. They are saying that we must not focus on cold outward institutional things, but on warm relational personal qualities. One famous theologian even said that a couple might be legally married but not really married because their personal relationship fell short of what it ought to be.

All this talk sounds very warm and personal. But it is actually disastrous, because marriage is an institution, not an ideal. If we think of marriage as an ideal towards which we strive, we replace the security of a God-given institution by the fragility of a human project. That is, in Bible terms, we take the whole thing out of the realm of grace and into the cold wilderness of trying to do it all on our own.

The reality is that marriage is a status that is entered, not an ideal towards which we aspire. It is a good institution, entered on the day a couple marry. And within that given institution, with its boundaries, they are called by God to live out their marriage. Within the security of the institution we may grow in safety and confidence; outside it we may strive, but always with that paralysing fear that we are on our own.

It is important to be clear that all this has nothing to do with church or church weddings. In Graham Greene's depressing novel *Brighton Rock*, the petty teenage gangster ('The Boy') wants to 'get married' to the girl who knows evidence against him, so that her evidence will be inadmissible in court. His lawyer asks him, 'Do you want to be married in a church?' 'Of course I don't,' he replies. 'This won't be a real marriage.' 'Real enough,' answers the lawyer. 'Not real like when the priest says it,' replies the boy. This idea that it is somehow more 'real . . . when the priest says it' is very common. But it is completely wrong and has no basis in the Bible.

There have been many different cultural ways to begin a marriage. Marriage has been dressed in many different kinds of cultural clothing, with all sorts of different ceremonies and customs. And that includes the Bible itself, which records all sorts of different marriage customs. Frankly, they don't matter a bit. Just because marriage has been entered using some particular customs in one culture doesn't mean we are bound always to enter marriage the same way. (Otherwise we should presumably have to begin every honeymoon in the tent of the bridegroom's mother, if we were to follow Isaac's example in Genesis 24:67!)

It doesn't matter whether a couple get married in church or elsewhere. It doesn't matter whether they have a grand and expensive reception or fish and chips in the local pub. It doesn't even matter whether they are Christians or not (for Christian marriage is not a different institution from marriage in general), so long as they actually get married. On that day they enter a God-given institution whose shape and boundaries are not up for negotiation. Marriage is what marriage is.

We have seen some of the problems and pain when the boundaries are broken. Let us now explore in more detail why these boundaries are given. Marriage may be simply defined as follows:

■ **Marriage is the voluntary public union of one man and one woman from different families.**

What are the boundaries?

Husband and wife must be from different families

I am not going to say much about the restriction that they should be from different families. If they are from the same family circle, the Bible calls it incest. The reason this is not allowed is to protect the order and security of the family circle. If a man and a woman, who are not husband and wife, live in the same family (or extended family, depending on the culture), then sex is off limits for ever, so that the family group can be kept free from the tensions and destructive confusion that sexual liaisons would introduce. We see this principle worked out in the culture of Old Testament Israel in Leviticus 18, and a New Testament example, of cohabitation with a stepmother, in 1 Corinthians 5:1. This is a very important boundary in the Bible, but I am not going to say more about it here.

One man marries one woman

Neither am I going to say much about the boundary that marriage is between one man and one woman. This means that it is heterosexual rather than homosexual, and that it is monogamous rather than polygamous. It is heterosexual because this is how God has made us, not least because we are designed for sex with children in mind. Because God has not made us for this, it is not surprising that homosexual practice carries with it serious medical dangers.

And it is to be monogamous, again because this is how God has made us. There is some polygamy in Old Testament cultures (though almost always only for kings or tribal chieftains), and it is recorded by the historians in passing. They often record morally dubious things without stopping to pass judgment on them, because they have a bigger story to tell. They do not pause to tell us 'that was good' or 'that was bad' about many actions they record.

But the Genesis account (Genesis 2) records one man and one woman. The horrible character of the first bigamist, Lamech, in Genesis 4:23–24 begins a tale in which polygamy is consistently associated with dysfunctional families. Monogamy is affirmed by Jesus (Mark 10:6–8), who draws attention to it when he says 'they are no longer *two*, but one flesh'. All this confirms that it was always God's purpose for marriage to be between one man and one woman.

I want to focus more carefully on the boundary restrictions that marriage is both voluntary and a publicly pledged commitment. We shall see that these two boundaries are closely related.

Marriage is a voluntary union

First, marriage is voluntary: a couple have to consent to get married. They must not be forced. A man and a woman may have chosen each other, or loving parents may have arranged the marriage and suggested it to them. Both are acceptable, so long as there is no coercion and they really do consent to marry. But what does it mean, to consent to marriage?

Of course, they must consent to sex. That ought to be

obvious. Rape is abhorred in the Bible as it ought to be everywhere. But to consent to sex is not the same as to consent to marriage. Prostitutes, adulterous lovers and cohabiting couples all consent to sex, but none of them have consented to be married. Consent to marriage means consenting to promise publicly exclusive lifelong faithfulness. It means saying in front of witnesses 'I . . . take you . . . to be my husband/wife'. It means to say this in the present tense: not 'I intend to take you . . .' (which would be betrothal or engagement), but 'I take you . . .'.

Consent to marriage means to understand and agree that each will be the only sexual partner of the other until one of them dies, and to have some understanding that this includes, if possible, openness to having children and the desire to build a home together. That is, it ought to mean agreeing to sex in the service of God, sex to build a faithful relationship, sex to create a new family unit, out of which they can become (in the old-fashioned phrase) a useful couple in society. This is God's purpose, even if in practice couples may not always realize it clearly.

The detail of this consent does not need to be spelt out word for word at each wedding; there are some things taken as understood in any culture. Nor does a couple need to be able to put it all fluently into words. Often it is taken for granted, although the more confused a culture, the more necessary it is to explain afresh what marriage means. One of the blessings of getting married in church is that we are clearly reminded of the meaning of marriage before the promises are made. But one way or another a couple need to agree to be married.

Marriage is a public union

And they need to do this publicly. Those who say that the rest of us ought not to interfere with 'what happens privately in the bedroom' are guilty of shallow thinking. For sexual relationships always touch others and have effects on wider society. Sex is never private in its effects. People sometimes say that the public dimension is a recent church idea, because people didn't get married 'in church' (or in the synagogue) in the Bible, and a marriage service in church is just a cultural idea.

But whatever the varied cultural ceremonies by which people enter marriage, at heart it has always been meant to be a public thing. Indeed, in the New Testament a 'marriage' means 'a marriage feast' (e.g. Matthew 22:2), a public celebration which is precisely the point at which the couple get married. They did not have the party at Cana *after* the marriage service; the public feast *was* the marriage event (John 2:1–11).

A couple do not gradually drift into a relationship and then retrospectively mark it with some sort of party later if they feel like it. Rather, they have a public celebration and that *is* the point at which they get married. Whatever precise words are used, it is understood by them and everybody else that on that day they become husband and wife.

Marriage begins with public consent not consummation

Of course, the expectation is that they will then consummate their marriage privately with sexual intercourse. But the order is important, because what the Bible calls 'nakedness' (meaning the nakedness of sexual intimacy) speaks of tremendous vulnerability. In sexual intimacy we open ourselves to another as in no other context in human life. And that vulnerability is safe only after first pledging lifelong faithfulness. Sex within marriage is to be sex in safety. Sex before or outside marriage is sex exposed to danger.

In fact marriage is defined by public consent and not by sexual consummation. A couple may sleep together and not be married. But if they make their public vows, then they are married, whether or not they then succeed in consummating the marriage. Marriage must begin when vows of consent are exchanged publicly. After that, neither husband nor wife can claim they are not married.

A marriage where the couple fail to have sexual intercourse

(for physical or psychological reasons) is still a marriage, albeit a sad and frustrating one. This is important, so that the vulnerabilities and fragility of learning sexual intimacy may take place within the secure context of knowing the promises have been firmly made. At no point in marriage do husband or wife need to *prove* anything by successful sex.

This is another way in which the marriage institution is a good gift of grace. For sex within marriage is sex under grace, with nothing to prove. A married couple may 'do well' or 'do badly' at sex, and cheerfully laugh about it knowing that their relationship is not threatened when they do badly. And even if the problems are too severe for them cheerfully to laugh, they can work patiently at them, knowing that the marriage does not depend on success in this area, but rather on the solemn public promises already made. For them, sex is 'under grace', within the security of promises made.

On the other hand, sex outside marriage is always sex 'under law' (as it were): always seeking to prove, always striving to do well enough to keep the other one in the relationship, always anxious lest at any time the other may decide there is not enough in it for them, always under trial.

Marriage is defined by public consent not private emotion

It is important to be clear that it is this public event that makes a couple married. And it is also important to be clear that the public giving of consent in the marriage vows *is* the consent of the two people concerned. Their private state of mind, whether or not they are having cold feet while saying them, is neither here nor there. By publicly saying these things they commit themselves to their public promises, no matter what muddles and uncertainties there may be in the backs of their minds, or what butterflies in their stomachs. A promise is a promise, and commits me to keeping it, whatever the cost. This is why the psalmist commends those who make promises and keep them even when it proves costly (Psalm 15:4).

In Thomas Hardy's novel *Far from the Madding Crowd*, Francis Troy stands beside the open coffin of his former lover Fanny and their infant child, in giving birth to whom Fanny had died. As Troy's wife Bathsheba comes up beside him, Troy kisses Fanny's cold lips. Bathsheba protests at this sign of affection to one who was merely his lover. Troy turns from her protest and says to Fanny, 'But never mind, darling, in the sight of Heaven you are my very, very wife!' Bathsheba asks in desperation, 'If she's – that, what – am I?' Troy replies, 'You are nothing to me – nothing. A ceremony before a priest doesn't make a marriage. I am not morally yours.' Troy is right that a ceremony before a priest doesn't make a marriage. But he is quite wrong in every other respect. What makes a marriage is publicly pledged faithfulness. And he had made that pledge to Bathsheba. Whatever his private emotions, in the sight of heaven Bathsheba was his wife, and he ought to have acknowledged it. The same sort of fraud is committed today when someone deserts a husband or wife for a lover, persuading themselves that in the sight of heaven this is their true destiny, because they have such strong feelings for their lover. But it is a fraud.

Why marriage is better than cohabitation

There are a number of other benefits of marriage over against its more flexible and supposedly more free alternatives in our culture.

Marriage is unambiguous
First, it is unambiguous. When a man and woman begin sleeping together and perhaps move in together, the rest of us are left guessing as to what exactly is the basis of their relationship. Clearly they have agreed to sleep together, as otherwise it would be rape. But what have they promised one

another, if anything? On what basis or shared understanding are they together?

The answers are as many as there are couples, ranging from very little commitment to a fair degree of privately promised commitment, sometimes expressed, for example, in a joint mortgage. But always there is ambiguity. Some research suggests that often the woman's expectations are higher than the man's. Typically the woman really thinks this is 'for keeps', whereas the man is a touch more cautious and waits to see how good it is, happy to enjoy the benefits while it's fun. Sometimes it may be the other way around. But always it is unclear. And therefore the rest of us do not know quite how to relate to them.

Nowhere is this ambiguity more painful than when one of them dies. Who is the next of kin? With whom should we grieve most deeply? The parents, or the live-in partner?

But in a marriage, there is no lack of clarity. Each has publicly pledged lifelong faithfulness to the other. They are next of kin from that day on. They have left their parents, in that fundamental sense (Genesis 2:24).

Marriage is a union of families; cohabitation is free-floating

Second, a marriage is a union of families rather than just of two free-floating individuals. I was on a train and overheard two young women speaking rather loudly (as people sometimes do on trains). One told the other about her moving in with her 'partner' and how she had later married him. 'I noticed,' she said, 'that my parents were much more involved with the wedding than with our living together.' This is not surprising. Because the 'moving in' was an attempt to keep the arrangement private. Not private in the sense of secret, but private in the sense of an arrangement agreed to and confined to the two of them, with families only rather awkwardly and ambiguously involved.

But a marriage is a joining of families, and – for all the stresses sometimes involved – this wider connection is a blessing. It is better to be connected than to float 'free' but disconnected from wider family and society. To float free of wider family connections is the sad freedom of Cain in the land of wandering (Genesis 4:16), or of the scattered peoples of Babel (Genesis 11:9). Scattering always speaks of a curse in the Bible, and gathering into a people and a family, of blessing. This is because God wants his world governed in an ordered way by connected people. Marriage is an expression of this on a local scale.

Marriage provides protection for the vulnerable at the start

Third, the public nature of marriage provides an important protection for the vulnerable at the start of the sexual relationship. We sometimes think that we are autonomous free-floating individuals who make decisions for ourselves. The reality is that we are influenced in many ways in every decision we make. And in the area of sex, above all, we are open to manipulation and exploitation, even unwittingly, by passions that rage and desires that can overwhelm us. We can be swept into all sorts of decisions we later regret.

The public and family nature of marriage provides some protection against this. This is why in history the churches have acted to safeguard couples against being pressured into secret marriages.

In Genesis 34 there is a strange incident usually called 'the rape of Dinah' (one of Jacob's daughters). However, it is not at all clear that Dinah was raped by Shechem, the son of the local Canaanite prince. It is quite likely that Shechem persuaded her to live with him, in something that fell short of physical coercion. We suspect this because he continues to love her fondly (verses 8, 19) in a way which would be most unusual for a rapist, and because she stays in his house for quite a long time (verse 26), and it seems unlikely she was simply kidnapped. Most likely, she was persuaded, as a young and vulnerable woman away from her family, to live with Shechem. What she needed was the protection of her family. In order to protect her, Shechem ought to have asked for the consent of her father before taking her into his home.

In rather the same way, because marriage is a public union in which the families ought to be involved, and not just the two individuals, it offers the protection and wisdom of families in a way that can protect the vulnerable from being exploited or making foolish decisions under the pressure of passion. It is common to despise the involvement of families as oppressive and a constraint on individual freedom. And it is true that families can behave badly. But more often, because the parents love their son or daughter, they will actually act in their best interests. The public nature of marriage encourages this.

Marriage offers some hope of justice to those wronged when it ends

Fourth, one important blessing of marriage is that it offers some real protection and justice for the one who is wronged when a marriage breaks up. When a man or woman walks out of a sexual relationship, the other partner always suffers. In marriage, however, society recognizes that the abandoned party has rights which the other needs to honour. And in a healthy society the one who walks out is forced to honour these rights and is not able to walk away irresponsibly. The courts may impose a settlement and perhaps insist on con-tributions towards the care of children. Even though this is not done perfectly, and there is still injustice, at least with marriage there is some social framework to try to ensure justice.

It is true that legislation seems gradually to be imposing obligations of justice on cohabiting partners. Perhaps before long no one will be able to walk out of a cohabitation without some obligation to fulfil responsibilities to the other (especially if there are children). We must welcome this. But we must also note that every move in this direction makes unmarried cohabitation less attractive to those who entered it precisely in order to avoid the obligations of marriage. Indeed, we could make a case for saying that society *ought* to treat cohabiting partners as if they were married, with all the obligations that entails. This would mean that to break a cohabitation, one party would have to sue for what would effectively be divorce! If that were to happen, then the mere action of moving in together would come to *signify* the commitment verbalized in the marriage vows, and then cohabitation would *mean* marriage. At the moment it does not. And until and unless it does, only marriage provides proper protection for the vulnerable.

Marriage strengthens private intentions with public promises

Fifth, the public promises of marriage are necessary because when we make public promises we lay our reputation and integrity on the line behind those promises. There is all the difference in the world between a fond promise made privately during a cuddle on the sofa ('Will you stay with me for ever?' 'Of course, darling, how could you ever imagine otherwise?') and a public promise made before witnesses in the cold light of day.

Private assurances are terribly easy to break; they evaporate like the morning dew. After all, it is only your word against mine when I say that you misunderstood me and I didn't really say or mean what you thought. We are deeply prone to self-deception in this area above all.

But when all my wider family, my friends, my work colleagues, and my neighbours know I have publicly made this pledge, then I am much more inclined to keep it. I do not want them thinking I am a liar. And marriage begins precisely with those public promises. It doesn't matter, incidentally, if the marriage ceremony is attended by only a few. The point is that my promises are witnessed by witnesses who represent the whole of the rest of society. To say 'I am married' means precisely that I have made these promises and all the world can know it.

So public promises, like the skins for clothing given to Adam and Eve (Genesis 3:21), are necessary because of human weakness. Someone has said that democracy is possible because human beings are capable of justice, but that democracy is necessary because we are also capable of injustice. That is, we couldn't create a democratic society without some sense of justice, and we need to create one to provide safeguards against injustice. In a similar way, we may say that our capacity for faithfulness makes marriage possible, but our capacity for unfaithfulness makes marriage necessary. We need the public promises to hold us to the faithfulness we pledge.

When we struggle in difficult marriages, it is a great help to know that we have publicly promised to be faithful for life, and that everybody else expects us to keep that promise, and that if we don't then we must expect to experience shame. All this strengthens and supports marriage, and helps us keep to the end the promises we made at the start.

Conclusion

In all these ways I hope we can see that the marriage institution is a creation blessing from God. It is one of the great 'givens' of the world, not flexible and open to negotiation, and it is given as a gift of grace. On the day a couple publicly pledge themselves to one another for life before witnesses they enter this gracious institution. They do not gradually grow into it. They enter it; and then within the secure boundaries of marriage they live out their calling as a married couple called to build a relationship of safe and overflowing love that brings order, blessing and fruitfulness in the connected context of wider family and society. In this way the proper boundaries and order of marriage serve God in his world.

For study or discussion

1. What words does the Bible use to make it clear that sex is for marriage alone?

2. How have social patterns changed to blur the marriage boundary?

3. What experience do you have of this in your family or circle of friends?

4. What does 'creation order' mean, and how is it different from the idea that each person or culture can invent its own 'right and wrong'?

5. How does Proverbs 5 show us that breaking the boundaries of marriage leads to misery? Have you seen this kind of misery in your family or circle of friends?

6. And what about Proverbs 6:20–35? Have you seen destructive jealousies causing misery in your family or circle of friends?

7. Why is it a relief that God has given us marriage in creation?

8. Why must husband and wife be from different families?

9. What event makes a man and woman married?

10. Why does it need to be public?

11. How does marriage protect sex and provide for sex an umbrella of grace?

12. Why is marriage better than cohabitation? How can you use these arguments to commend marriage to others?

7 Is it better to stay single?

Jack was twenty-two and raring to serve God with heart, mind, soul and strength. His zeal was almost frightening. Jack was also a hot-blooded male. His body and heart told him he really must find a Christian girl and marry her – and just as soon as he decently could! But he had just heard a really inspiring talk from a veteran missionary, an unmarried man, who had spent forty-five years doing pioneering cross-cultural work in Papua New Guinea amongst unreached tribespeople. It was an amazing story of sacrifice, hardship and perseverance. Something stirred in Jack's heart.

And then the next week one of the church leaders gave a talk to the twenties group from 1 Corinthians 7, about how Paul held up singleness as better than marriage, for those who really wanted to serve God wholeheartedly.

Lisa had heard both those same talks too. So when Jack later, and rather tentatively, asked her out, both of them felt faintly guilty, with just that nagging feeling in the backs of their minds that they might be settling for God's second best. They were strongly attracted to each other. They knew God had invented marriage. And yet...

Our motto has been 'sex in the service of God'. But what about 'no-sex in the service of God'? Isn't there a place for that? Indeed, in Christian history there has been an honoured place. This book is about marriage rather than singleness. It is for singles thinking about getting married, for engaged couples preparing for marriage, and for married couples seeking to build good marriages. So being unmarried is not our subject.

But I need at this point to address a question asked by some singles. If I am concerned about serving God, might it not be the case that I can love and serve God better unmarried? Because if I can, then maybe I should give marriage a miss, and live a life of greater usefulness as a single man or woman?

This attitude is in refreshing contrast to a society which seems to think that we cannot be fully human without having sex. Even within our churches, it is unusual to have a positive view of the unmarried state. This is an irony for a religion whose founder never married and one of whose most significant apostles (Paul) did his pioneering missionary work as an unmarried man.

There is really only one thing that absolutely needs to be said: the whole duty and calling of every human being who has ever lived is to love God with heart, mind, soul and strength. This is true for children and adults, men and women, marrieds and singles, for every race, language and culture. This is the one absolute human obligation and calling every day of every life. We must love God.

The only question is *how* we are going to love and serve God. And this is where marriage does make quite a difference. So let us explore the difference. Four things need to be said.

Sex makes no difference to our relationship with God

Sex does not matter. It is very important to say this loudly in a society which thinks sex matters a lot. Neither the married nor the unmarried state is higher in any absolute spiritual sense. It is not more spiritual to be single, nor is it more spiritual to be married. Old Testament religion bent over backwards to keep clear blue water between it and the Canaanite religions, in which sex had religious significance. The priests and Levites were generally married, like everybody else. The only difference was that the rules for their marriages were just that bit stricter to avoid even a suspicion of sexual misconduct. Among the apostles, Peter was married (Matthew 8:14–15) and others (1 Corinthians 9:5). All this is of no religious significance.

Sex is not to be compulsory, as in Canaanite religion. But neither is it to be forbidden, as Paul makes clear in 1 Timothy 4:3 and also in 1 Corinthians 7:1–6 (where Paul vigorously disagrees with the suggestion that it is good for a man not to have sex with his wife). In terms of a person's standing with God, therefore, it makes not a scrap of difference whether they are married or single.

We find our identity and experience love within the family of God

Not only does sex have no significance so far as getting close to God is concerned; neither is it the only way we find fulfilment or friendship for ourselves in this age. We have seen in chapter 2 that marriage is not God's answer to loneliness, but that we are to experience love and belonging in the context of fellowship with God and fellow Christians.

The single need not be lonely if our churches are fellowships of inclusive love. 'Single' ought not to mean 'solitary'. The unmarried ought not to be 'singles' floating around the world alone, but rather – like the marrieds – men and women who belong in loving communities and fellowships, the family of God. If they are lonely that may be because our church fellowships are not functioning properly to include them in natural warm fellowship and friendships. So often we hear of singles who are rarely invited to family meals or dinners, because it is always couples who are asked. This ought not to be.

Because sex has no religious significance and does not define our identity, a husband should avoid speaking of his wife, or a wife of her husband, as 'my other/better half'. This is often said light-heartedly, but it promotes an understanding that without him or her I am only half a person. The world thinks this is so, but Christians ought to bend over backwards to avoid ever agreeing with them, even in jest.

Some will endure not being married for the sake of God's kingdom

[11]But he [Jesus] said to them, 'Not everyone can receive this saying, but only those to whom it is given. [12]For there are eunuchs who have been so from birth, and there are eunuchs who have been made eunuchs by men, and there are eunuchs who have made themselves eunuchs for the sake of the kingdom of heaven. Let the one who is able to receive this receive it.'
(Matthew 19:11–12)

However, even though the unmarried need not be lonely, the fact remains that not to be married is for most people a costly deprivation. I use the word 'deprivation' deliberately. The Bible recognizes what we know in everyday experience: that sexual desires are right and natural. By sexual desires, I mean much more than just the intense physical longings, but also all the common and natural desires for marriage, home and family. Not to be able to satisfy these longings is a costly deprivation that usually hurts a lot.

Jesus used the shocking word 'eunuch' when speaking about this, and taught that 'there are eunuchs who have been so from birth, and there are eunuchs who have been made so by men, and there are eunuchs who have made themselves eunuchs for the sake of the kingdom of heaven' (Matthew 19:12). Some are incapable of marriage by some physical or psychological incapacity they have had from birth. Others are incapacitated for marriage by something that happens to them: something in their nurture, perhaps, or their circumstances that prevents them from marrying. It may be simply that they never meet anyone suitable who wants to marry them. For whatever human reason, they do not marry.

And then there is a third category. Jesus gives three examples, but not because all three are equal in significance. He gives three so that the first two can build up to the third. (This is a familiar form in the Old Testament Wisdom literature. We saw it in Proverbs 30:18–19 earlier, where the first three things are the build-up to the fourth.) Jesus' emphasis is on this third category, because it is so shocking. The first two are, I suppose, fairly obvious (though of course sad). But his main point is the shocking one that for the sake of the kingdom of God some people voluntarily endure this deprivation; they deprive themselves of this natural blessing and the fulfilment of these natural desires. Jesus could have put this more softly simply by saying, 'some do not marry . . .', but he chose to use the horrifying metaphor of castration, to emphasize the costliness and pain of this choice. His point is that, though marriage is good, remaining unmarried is sometimes necessary, as it was for him.

When Jesus finishes his saying about 'eunuchs' with, 'Let the one who is able to receive this receive it', we need to be clear what he means. It is unlikely that he means that only to some is given the spiritual gift of renouncing marriage, and that unless someone feels happy and comfortable with this choice, it is probably not for them. To 'receive' or 'make room for' a truth typically means to make room for the truth about Jesus. It is what a disciple does and what the world cannot do. The challenge to receive a truth is parallel to the challenge 'Let anyone with ears to hear, hear.' So all disciples ought to receive this truth Jesus teaches.

If this were a truth that some could comfortably and easily accept because they were happy to be single, the metaphor of the eunuch would be very inappropriate. The point is that all disciples need to make room in their thinking for the shocking possibility of not getting married, costly and painful though that would be. To be a disciple of Jesus means to put Jesus and his gospel and his kingdom absolutely first, above all else.

All unmarried disciples ought to be open to this choice, because they understand how urgent and vital is the work of the kingdom of God.

This is a particular example of a more general truth, which is that the time of perfect happiness and fulfilment is not yet. Between Jesus' earthly life and his resurrection lay his cross. Between our present lives and our resurrection bodies lies a life of discipleship in which we are called to take up the cross and follow him. We are to expect costs in discipleship. Loyalty to Jesus must come before loyalty even to our closest family (e.g. Luke 14:26; 18:29–30).

So, while we understand that sex in itself is of no significance in bringing us closer to God, or taking us further from God, we also need to make space in our thinking for the costly fact that some disciples will renounce marriage for the sake of the kingdom.

Getting married makes life a lot more complicated!

If people think they can serve God better unmarried, it is probably because of what Paul teaches in 1 Corinthians 7. It is very important to be clear what Paul is saying, and not saying, in his lengthy teaching about the married and un-married states in this chapter. We focus here only on whether or not he thinks we can serve God better unmarried.

We must remember first (as we have seen in chapter 4) that in verses 1–6 Paul shows himself clearly in favour of marriage, and of regular sex within marriage. Paul was never an ascetic, someone who thought deprivation was good for its own sake. And he was not hostile to sex (as we saw in 1 Corinthians 7:2–5). He himself may well have been married (as just about all rabbis had to be) and subsequently widowed. And although he is not married now (as we know from verse 8, and from 1 Corinthians 9:5), he no doubt experiences sexual temptation like anybody else. And in general he thinks it is for the best if men and women get married and then have regular sex within marriage.

What does the 'gift' of singleness mean?

> I wish that all were as I myself am. But each has his own gift from God, one of one kind and one of another.
> (1 Corinthians 7:7)

But then, surprisingly, in verse 7 he says, 'I wish that all were as I myself am [that is, unmarried]. But each has his own gift from God, one of one kind and one of another.' What is this 'gift', whether of marriedness or of singleness?

It is a common misunderstanding to think that I know whether I have the gift of singleness by whether or not I *feel* happy to be single. It is often said that only if I am quite content to be unmarried and really experience no strong sexual urges or other desires for marriage, only then can I say I have this gift. And if I don't feel content like this, then I should get married if I can.

This idea that the gift equates to the desire is wrong, for two reasons. First, if we apply the same reasoning the other way around, it makes a nonsense of marriage. With this approach, someone discerns whether he has the gift of marriedness by whether or not he is happy and content to be married. So let us suppose someone is married, but is struggling in a difficult marriage and is, frankly, not at all content in his marriedness. Does he conclude that he does not have the gift of marriedness, and go ahead and get a divorce? That would be absurd, quite apart from being forbidden in verses 10 and 11.

The second reason we know this is wrong is this: what happens if someone feels he has the gift of marriage but no suitable opportunity comes along? Is he to conclude that a good and gracious God has given him the 'gift' of marriage but then carelessly forgotten to make marriage possible for him? This again would be absurd.

No, I know which 'gift' I have by a very simple test: if I am married, I have the gift of marriage; if I am not married, I have the gift of being unmarried. My circumstances are God's gracious gift to me, and I am to learn to accept them from his hand as such.

At the time of writing this I happen to be married. So I know I have the gift from God of being married, and I am to accept my state as the gift of God to me and to learn contentment in it (even when it is difficult). I may not always be married, as my wife may die before I do. If she does, then in my grief I will need to accept my new unmarried state equally as God's gracious gift to me, and to learn contentment in it. This will be very hard, just as it is hard for some singles to learn contentment in their unmarried state.

So we must not slip into thinking 'Once I have the gift, I will always have this same gift.' Not at all. All of us have the gift of being single for the first two or three decades of life. Half of us will end our lives with the gift of singleness (because we will be widowed). Most of us have a time in between when we have the gift of being married, though some do not. But all of us at every stage need to learn contentment as we accept what we are now as the gracious gift of a good God.

It is better to get married than to have sex outside marriage

8To the unmarried and the widows I say that it is good for them to remain single as I am. 9But if they cannot exercise [literally 'are not exercising'] self-control, they should marry. For it is better to marry than to be aflame with passion.
(1 Corinthians 7:8–9)

So, as an unmarried man who is learning contentment, Paul goes on in verses 8–9 to address 'the unmarried' (men, possibly widowers) and 'the widows'. He says 'that it is *good'* for them to remain single as he is. But if they are not exercising self-control, they should marry. 'For it is better to marry than to be aflame with passion.' Self-control is always important, and sexual intimacy outside marriage is always wrong and damaging. This battle for purity of body and mind is one that every Christian is called to fight. Paul is not saying that sexual intimacy outside marriage is ever right. What he is saying is that if marriage is available (and of course often it isn't), the Christian is free to marry and may well be wise to marry, especially if his or her sexual desires are strong.

If this is so – and it makes perfect practical sense – we need to ask why Paul thinks there is anything to be said on the other side: that is, in favour of not getting married. For, on the face of it, for most of us, it would seem to be a 'no-brainer': we ought to get married as soon as we can! The reason it may be better not to marry (or marry again after being widowed) is not because it is spiritually higher not to marry, but because to remain single will keep our lives simpler (as we shall see below).

Verses 10–16 address a different question, of divorce, which is outside the scope of this book. Verses 17–24 teach that we are to accept our condition (in this case, married or unmarried) as the circumstances in which God has called us, and to learn contentment. As a wise pastor, Paul knows how unsettling it can be to be constantly discontented, always wanting to be in different circumstances, even thinking that 'if only' we were different, then we could walk more closely with God. Not at all, he says, don't worry about your present situation, but learn contentment in it. And don't think that a change in your marital status will bring about a change in your spiritual life.

Verses 25–31 introduce a new topic (verse 25 'concerning the betrothed', literally, 'concerning virgins'). The question is whether those who are engaged ought to go ahead and get married. It is a paradoxical section. The main point seems to be that because we are on the edge of the age to come, we ought not to be too tightly attached in our affections to this age. They lived in 'the present distress' (verse 26), which may have been something specific to Corinth then (probably times of famine), or may be a general reference to the last days, in which we still live. And because of that distress, getting married (which would usually mean having children) is likely to make life harder. And so, as a caring pastor, he warns them not to jump lightly into this trouble. Again, we see the word 'good', as in verse 8: 'it is good for a person to remain as he is'. This does not mean that it puts him or her on a spiritually higher plane, closer to God. It means that there are practical benefits to remaining as you are. He says that the unmarried state may be better for their sake, not for God's sake. His reasons are pastoral. And this leads on to his pastoral concern in the next section.

Marriage can make us anxious!

[32]I want you to be free from anxieties. The unmarried man is *anxious* about the things of the Lord, how to please the Lord. [33]But the married man is *anxious* about worldly things, how to please his wife, [34]and his interests are divided. And the unmarried or betrothed woman is *anxious* about the things of the Lord, how to be holy in body and spirit. But the married

woman is *anxious* about worldly things, how to please her
husband. [35]I say this for your own benefit, not to lay any
restraint upon you, but to promote good order and to secure
your undivided devotion to the Lord.
(1 Corinthians 7:32–35, my emphases)

Verses 32–35 are a very important and easily misunderstood
section, which we need to consider with care. Paul begins in
verse 32 by saying, 'I want you to be free from anxieties', and
ends in verse 35 that he writes 'not to lay any restraint' on them,
but is writing 'for your own benefit'. He is not writing to teach
some great spiritual principle, but as a pastor with practical
guidance to free them from anxious care. Four times he uses
the word 'care' (or 'anxious care'): in verses 32, 33 and 34 (twice).
He wants them, and us, to go away from this passage with a
new spring in our step. And (verse 35) he wants to secure their
'undivided devotion to the Lord'.

The anxiety he has in mind is the care of the conscientious
Christian, who can feel torn apart by apparently irreconcilable
things that he or she ought to do. She wakes in the morning and
thinks, 'What ought I to do today?' Perhaps there are elderly
parents to care for. Perhaps there are children to parent, a
home to manage, even a garden to tend (so that it doesn't
become like the sluggard's garden in Proverbs 24:30–31!),
budgets to watch, friendships to maintain, responsibilities in a
job, and church obligations as well. No wonder she (or he) feels
anxious. The more conscientious the Christian is, the worse
this becomes. If I just live for myself, it is no big problem. But if
I take my responsibilities seriously, then it is a problem and
perhaps a cause of stress.

Paul says, 'I want you to be free from anxieties.' And the
particular issue he has in mind is whether or not to get married.
In what he says next he simplifies, so as to focus on this
question. He draws a contrast, first for the man, and then for
the woman: the same contrast, repeated for emphasis.

1. 'The unmarried man is anxious about the things of the Lord, how to please the Lord.'
2. 'But the married man is anxious about worldly things, how to please his wife, and his interests are divided.'
3. 'And the unmarried or betrothed woman [i.e. who is thinking about getting married] is anxious about the things of the Lord, how to be holy in body and spirit.'
4. 'But the married woman is anxious about worldly things, how to please her husband.'

On the face of it, Paul accuses the marrieds of worldliness. But this cannot be right. If getting married guarantees that it is no longer *possible* for me to love God with all my heart – if by getting married I make 'undivided devotion to the Lord' impossible – then it would necessarily follow that to get married is sin, and I ought not to do it (and Paul ought not to be in favour of it in verse 2). So he cannot mean this.

Let's go back to first principles for a moment. When Jesus summarizes the law of God he says, 'You shall love the Lord your God with all your heart and with all your soul and with all your mind. This is the great and first commandment. And a second is like it: You shall love your neighbour as yourself' (Matthew 22:37–39).

These are not two parallel commandments. We often think they are. We think that Jesus tells us to do an impossible balancing act: on the one hand, love God with everything you've got, but, on the other, make sure you don't forget to love your neighbour pretty wholeheartedly too! Keep up your religious obligation to love God; but keep it in balance with your social and moral obligation to love your fellow human beings. That would be impossible. No, there is one great commandment. The second is simply the practical expression of the first in daily life. As an expression of love for God I love the neighbour he sets in front of me. My love for neighbour is not in tension with my love for God, but the expression of it.

In particular, for married people, love for husband or wife is precisely an important expression of their love for God. For me to love my wife is not a distraction from loving God, but precisely what the God I love calls me to do. So the concern of the married man to please his wife is not at all an ungodly concern; it is precisely what he is told to do in Ephesians 5:25. And the concern of a married woman to please her husband is exactly what she is told to do in Titus 2:4. So 'worldly things' here cannot mean 'wrong things'. No, all the anxieties here are right and good anxieties, a desire to do the will of God.

What is more, even the unmarried man or woman cannot simply be 'devoted to the Lord' in some 'unworldly' sense. For he or she also may have elderly parents, neighbours in need, work responsibilities, and so on. So Paul is simplifying to make a point (rather as he does in verses 29–31). The point he is making is that getting married makes life a lot *more* complicated even than it would have been before! It is neither right nor wrong, but it will change your life, and you need to realize that and go into it with open eyes.

It is true that marriage complicates our lives. I had to speak on this subject at a conference some years ago. As I prepared the talks, my wife had to go away at short notice because her dear mother had died, and I was juggling four small children, school runs, and, as it happened, sports days, all with a team coming and going in our Rectory preparing for 190 people invited to lunch in the Rectory garden, and on top of the usual work of leading a church. When in desperation one night I set the alarm for 5.00 am to prepare my talk, we had an enormous thunderstorm at 3.00 am and our six-year-old snuggled into bed with me for a couple of hours, during which time she was sick three times. I was certainly anxious about doing all I was committed to do. Most of those anxieties would not have happened had I not got married (though I dare say I would still have had the 190 come to lunch!).

One mother of three in our last church was asked at a job interview, 'How would you feel if you had to try to do several things at once?' I hope she bit her tongue rather than lash out at her stupid (male) questioner, but I am pretty sure I know what she thought: doing several things at once is my normal life at home!

Paul's point is not that getting married is any better or any worse for serving God. It is simply that it introduces into our lives an enormous new complexity. Our moral obligations, the ways we love God, are now worked out in a multiplicity of different ('divided') ways. This is not wrong. But it is more complicated, and it may cause us stress. Not only do we 'take on' a husband or wife for whom we must care; we also now have to relate to their family. And, if we have children, then for the rest of our lives we will have responsibilities as parents and perhaps grandparents. All this is good. None of it is in principle ungodly. All of it ought to come under our motto of 'sex in the service of God'. But the *way* we serve God will necessarily be different now, and we cannot turn back the clock and choose to serve God in some other way. Paul writes to those considering marriage. As a pastor, he wants in love to warn them to go into it with open eyes, because it will make their lives more complicated. And therefore in some sense it may be more of a challenge for them to learn to love God with undivided devotion, although, thank God, it must still be possible.

We are free to marry or not

> [36]If anyone thinks that he is not behaving properly toward his betrothed, if his passions are strong, and it has to be, let him do as he wishes: let them marry – it is no sin. [37]But whoever is firmly established in his heart, being under no necessity but having his desire under control, and has determined this in his heart, to keep her as his betrothed, he will do well. [38]So then he

who marries his betrothed does well, and he who refrains from marriage will do even better.

(1 Corinthians 7:36–38)

In verses 36–38 Paul vigorously defends Christian freedom in this area. These verses contain one or two puzzles, which we cannot address here. But, in a nutshell, Paul says: you choose. Decide in your own mind what to do. It will be good to marry. And in some ways it will be even better not to, simply because it may save you anxiety and stress. It is not 'better' in a spiritual sense that it makes you a better Christian or brings you closer to God, but it may be 'better' *for you*, saving you trouble and stress. But it is entirely up to you. I am not going to tell you what to do. (And please don't join a church where the leaders do tell you what to do in this sort of matter!)

Conclusion: Can I serve God better unmarried?

So, can I serve God better unmarried? The general answer is no: neither better nor worse, but certainly differently. You will certainly serve God *differently* if you are married. For you will then be working with the motto, '*sex* (and everything that grows out of that heart of intimacy) in the service of God'. You will devote your energies and desires to building a relationship of faithfulness that is a model and image of Christ's love for his church, a love that overflows to others in loving service. God willing, you will devote your energies to the birth, growth and godly nurture of children. And all this will take it out of you.

There will therefore be other ways in which you will not be able to serve God, but the unmarried will. Those other ways of serving need to be done. Some people need to do them, especially perhaps some ministries that involve endless travel, or some particular kinds of pioneering cross-cultural missionary work.

And for some, therefore, it will mean the costly and painful loss of marriage, sex, and human family. We should respect and pray for those who make this choice, and those for whom this choice is made, for whatever reason. We should pray that they will exercise sexual self-control and learn contentment outside marriage, as we ask them to pray for the marrieds that we too will exercise sexual self-control within marriage and learn contentment in our marriages. Neither is an easy option.

When we have the choice as to whether or not to get married, this is a matter of Christian freedom. Let no one tell you what decision to take. So long as your proposed husband or wife shares your faith, if you are a Christian, and so long as he or she is willing to marry you, you are free to marry. You will not be closer to God if you do, and you will be no closer to God if you don't. You will not necessarily serve God better if you do, and you will not serve God better if you don't, but you will most certainly serve God differently.

For study or discussion

1. Think of the best unmarried role models you know.
   a. What have you learned from them?

   b. How are they serving God?

   c. In what ways do they serve God that would be difficult or impossible if they were married (and especially if they had children)?

2. Do the same exercise thinking of the best married role models you know.

3. a. How does our society treat those not in sexual relationships?

    b. How do churches sometimes treat single people?

    c. How can married people make sure they treat unmarried people better?

4. In what ways is the choice not to be married a costly one:
    a. Sexually, in our society?

    b. Socially, in the workplace and in church?

    c. From a family point of view?

5. Why, practically, do some need to make this costly choice for the sake of the kingdom?

6. a. What does it mean to have a gift from God of being single?

    b. And what does it not mean?

c. If you are married, how will understanding this change your attitude to singles?

7. What does it mean to have a gift from God of being married?

8. a. What reasons does Paul give to get married?

  b. And what reasons not to get married?

9. a. How does getting married make life more complicated?

  b. How can a married person still have undivided (and carefree) devotion to the Lord?

  c. How can an unmarried person do the same?

10. Try to think practically in terms of the reality of your life and the lives of married and unmarried people you know.
  a. How do we guard Christian freedom in our churches, when it comes to decisions to marry or not?

  b. Where does wise pastoral guidance end and coercion begin?

8 What is the heart of marriage?

Carl knew he had made a mistake. A big mistake. He had married Sally five years ago, and for the first year or so it had been OK. But as time went on it had become very clear to him that they were not compatible. They didn't communicate well. They often rubbed each other up the wrong way. Recently they had quarrelled a lot. In fact Carl dreaded going home, and used to postpone it as long as he decently could.

Last week Carl had got hold of a Christian book about marriage, which included lists of positive and negative points to help singles decide whether someone was well suited to them. He looked down the list and realized that he and Sally scored very, very low. If only he had seen those lists before they married, he would never have married her. It had been a terrible mistake. He felt pretty desperate about it, because he was a Christian and knew his church would disapprove when he and Sally split up.

But what could he do? After all, marriage *is* about love, he told himself. And although I used to love Sally, our love has died and I don't love her any more. I'm not sure there is anything I can do about that, he reasoned. It's very sad, but these things just happen. He began to rehearse his little speech of explanation to his minister...

Faithfulness is the heart of marriage, because it is the heart of God

The heart of marriage is the heart of the universe. If that sounds a bit grand for you, read on. So far we have mostly been asking the 'why?' question: what is the point of sex and marriage? We have been working with our motto, 'sex in the service of God'. In the course of doing that we have seen some answers to the question 'what?' and looked at the boundaries and shape of marriage. And yet to study the boundaries, however good they are, is rather like walking around the moat and walls of a castle without ever exploring the glory of the castle itself: faithfulness.

The heart of marriage is faithfulness. It is better to call it that than 'love', for love is too wishy-washy a term in popular use. Sometimes by 'love' we may convey something not a lot deeper than pink or blue heart symbols and romance. Often it is a word that speaks of feelings and desires rather than of commitment. So we will speak of faithfulness, or better still, of faithful love, or 'steadfast love', which is the best translation of an important Old Testament word for the love of the Covenant God. We see this wonderfully described in Exodus 34:6.

> The LORD, the LORD, a God merciful and gracious, slow to anger, and abounding in steadfast love and faithfulness...
> (Exodus 34:6)

The context is a time of terrible unfaithfulness on the part of God's people. In this context Moses hears this description of God: 'The LORD, the LORD, a God merciful and gracious,

slow to anger and abounding in *steadfast love and faithfulness* . . . '
No description of God is echoed as often as this one is in the
Bible. Faithful steadfast love is the heart of marriage, for faithful
steadfast love is the heart of the universe. The faithful steadfast
passionate Lover God calls men and women to show faithful
steadfast passionate love in their marriages.

This has little or nothing to do with 'falling' in (or out of)
love. We often speak of falling in love, or falling out of love,
both in society and – all too often – in the church.

One Christian marriage course includes in its publicity this
statement:

> Relationships begin when you fall in love. Relationships end
> when you no longer feel in love. So love is central, but it is
> rarely fully understood. The course will show how you can each
> give and receive the love you need. It will show you how to
> keep romance permanently alive.

A more Christian advertisement might read:

> *Marriage* begins when you publicly promise *lifelong faithfulness*.
> Marriage ends when one of you dies. *Faithfulness* is central, but it
> is rarely understood. The course will show you what faithfulness
> means and how to be faithful through good times and bad, no
> matter how you feel. It will show you how to keep *faithfulness*
> alive.

That would be a good deal less in tune with the age in which
we live, but a great deal more in tune with the Bible.

Marriage is a 'one flesh' union joined by God

[2]And Pharisees came up and in order to test [Jesus] asked, 'Is it
lawful for a man to divorce his wife?' [3]He answered them,

'What did Moses command you?' [4]They said, 'Moses allowed a man to write a certificate of divorce and to send her away.' [5]And Jesus said to them, 'Because of your hardness of heart he wrote you this commandment. [6]But from the beginning of creation, "God made them male and female." [7]"Therefore a man shall leave his father and mother and hold fast to his wife, [8]and they shall become one flesh." So they are no longer two but one flesh. [9]What therefore God has joined together, let not man separate.'

(Mark 10:2–9)

The Bible teaches us the centrality of faithfulness in two important ways. First, Genesis teaches that marriage is a union in which a couple become 'one flesh'. Jesus says that this means they are joined by God. This was the punchline of Jesus' teaching on marriage when he was asked about divorce in Mark 10 and Matthew 19. Quoting from Genesis 2:24, he said, ' "Therefore a man shall leave his father and mother and hold fast to his wife, and they shall become one flesh." So they are no longer two but one flesh. What therefore God has joined together, let not man separate' (Mark 10:7–9). Marriage involves leaving parents, so that husband and wife become 'next of kin' to one another. It involves a 'cleaving' or 'holding fast', a word which combines passion with permanence. And it results in a 'one flesh' union, which is a joining done by God.

Every married couple is joined by God

It is important to be clear that this applies to every married couple without exception, so long as they are validly married. It doesn't matter whether they have been married in church or not, or even in a Christian culture or not; for the church building, the Christian minister, and the Christian culture do not add anything essential to the marriage. The Bible shows no interest in the precise ceremonies or celebrations that begin married life. For example we are simply told that 'Isaac brought

[Rebekah] into the tent of Sarah his mother [who had died previously] and took Rebekah, and she became his wife' (Genesis 24:67). Jacob married Leah at a feast in which he apparently wasn't even quite sure whom he had married until the following morning (Genesis 29:22–25)! The marriage feast at Cana (John 2) did not follow after a synagogue service; the feast *was* the marriage and probably included some simple vows. Where a couple have agreed by public promises to take one another as husband and wife, God joins them together. They may be of a different religion or none; they may or may not be what we judge 'compatible'; the marriage may even be a marriage of convenience; but if they publicly consent to be married, then they are joined by God.

This is very important. We must not fall for the subjective idea that 'joining by God' is something that happens gradually as a marriage relationship grows, a kind of glue that slowly sets over time under the right conditions. In this case, the minister in a church wedding ought to replace Jesus' words by saying, 'I therefore declare that you may or may not grow into being joined by God. I hope you will, but we can never quite be sure.' This would be absurd and quite wrong.

If we think this joining by God is a gradual process, then it ruins the point Jesus is making. Jesus is speaking to the Pharisees, who thought divorce was an easy and legitimate way to end their marriages. They thought they could divorce and remain in God's 'good books' as respectable religious leaders. Jesus presses home to them and to us that we cannot do this, because our marriages are joined by God. He wants to stop us breaking our marriages.

But if a particular marriage may or may not be joined by God (depending how well the 'process' is getting on), then I can simply claim that my particular marriage hadn't managed to be joined by God and therefore I am quite justified in breaking it. This would make nonsense of Jesus' teaching. No, every properly married couple is joined by God.

'One flesh' union means a new family unit

To be joined by God is the same as what Genesis means by being 'one flesh'. This definition of marriage is affirmed by Jesus and echoed by Paul (Ephesians 5:31). What does 'one flesh' mean? It means a new family unit, built around the faithful and exclusive sexual union of husband and wife. To speak of another person as being of your 'flesh' is a normal way of recognizing a fellow family member (e.g. Genesis 29:14). God's purpose for sex is to make this new family unit by marriage a unit to be used by God in loving service in his world. This is why Paul tells the men in Corinth not to go to prostitutes (1 Corinthians 6:12–20). For to have sex with a prostitute is to do something that is intended by God to make the two of you a new family unit. But that is not at all your intention when you go to a prostitute. And therefore you are using sex for a very different purpose from God's purpose, and you ought not to do this.

So 'one flesh' means more than sex. But we need to be careful not to go to the opposite extreme. Sometimes people speak as though a 'one flesh' union means some deep psychological union (sometimes called 'total personal union'). Marriage is certainly meant to be a personal union, rather than just the satisfaction of animal appetites. But it is not 'full' or 'total' personal union, and if we think it is we are bound to be disappointed. Indeed, as has been noticed by poets and writers, there is always a frustration to sexual union, a sense that one has hardly begun to get to know the other as one might have hoped. Happily, 'one flesh' simply doesn't mean this. If we expect in marriage to achieve 'total personal union' with our husband or wife, it places on our marriage an impossible burden. Because if at any time our marriages don't feel very much like 'total personal union' (as any marriage doesn't quite a lot of the time, if we are honest), then we will be bound to worry that our marriages aren't working properly. But 'one flesh' doesn't mean some unattainable or fictitious psychological union. So let us free ourselves from these wrong and fanciful expectations. 'One flesh' simply means a new family unit.

We must not tear apart what God has joined

Jesus says that the point of the 'one flesh' union is that God joins it together and therefore no human being is permitted to tear it apart. It is right that in church weddings the words 'Those whom God has joined let no one put asunder' have pride of place. It is rather like when a child builds a beautiful balsa wood model. It is glued together and sits on the table to be admired. And then out of spite a nasty brother or sister throws it on the ground and breaks it. This is what we do when we break a marriage: we tear apart something potentially beautiful made by God.

Tragically, it is possible for human beings to tear apart what God has joined. Incidentally, it is a remarkable sign of the humility of God that he allows us to do this. We see this in another context in 1 Corinthians 3:16–17, where Paul calls the local church 'God's temple', God's building enterprise. He speaks of some who might 'destroy' God's temple, by acting divisively against the truth. He does not say they cannot destroy it; but he warns them that if they do, they make God their enemy ('If anyone destroys God's temple, God will destroy him.') In the same way, we can destroy God's building project of marriage, but if we do, we have God against us. Jesus says that we must not pull apart what God has joined together. This is not the unforgivable sin, but it is a very serious sin. Those who are the active agents in breaking a marriage need to repent and ask for the forgiveness that is available only in the Lord Jesus Christ.

This means that neither husband nor wife must tear their marriage apart. Neither of them is to put their career, comfort, personal fulfilment, or their own desires ahead of their marriage. If they do, they have God against them. Instead we must do all we can to nourish and build up our marriages, because they are unions made by God.

This also means that parents must not tear apart the marriages of their children, by being tiresomely interfering or by not giving them space to grow together and to form a new family unit. Parents must understand that their son or daughter has, in a vital sense, left them. Not that the son or daughter ceases to love them, to be loyal to them, to honour them, to care for them in old age, and so on, but they have left their childhood home and their parents are no longer their next of kin. Interfering parents have been sadly instrumental in the deaths of a number of marriages, and we must not do this. If we do, we have God against us.

Further, it means that no employer or person in a position of power ought to do anything to damage the marriages of their employees or juniors. They may do this by flirting or seductive behaviour in the workplace, or by imposing needlessly unsocial hours or punitive work hours, in a persistent way that erodes and gradually destroys marriages. I was speaking to one friend who used to be in a particular profession, until his boss explicitly said to him that if he was going to make a success of that profession he needed to put his career ahead of his marriage. He is now in another occupation, and rightly so. Those who exploit their power like that boss have God against them.

Marriage is a covenant to which God is witness

[13]And this second thing you do. You cover the LORD's altar with tears, with weeping and groaning because he no longer regards the offering or accepts it with favour from your hand. [14]But you say, 'Why does he not?' Because the LORD was witness between you and the wife of your youth, to whom you have been faithless, though she is your companion and your wife by covenant.
(Malachi 2:13–14)

The second way the Bible shows us that faithfulness is the heart of marriage is by calling it a covenant to which God is witness. We find this most clearly in the prophet Malachi. Malachi speaks to God's people perhaps four or so centuries before Jesus, at a time when they were complacent and unfaithful in a number of ways. One of the problems appears to have been that, as so often, unfaithfulness to God carried over into unfaithfulness in marriages. So in Malachi 2:13 the people complain that God won't pay attention to their religion. And in verse 14 the prophet tells them why not: 'Because the LORD was witness between you and the wife of your youth, to whom you have been faithless, though she is your companion and wife by covenant.' The expression 'the wife of your youth' echoes Proverbs 5:18, where the young husband is encouraged to go on taking sexual delight in 'the wife of [his] youth'. She is his 'companion': that is, joined to him, his friend, the one who goes through life with him. And she is his 'wife by covenant'.

A covenant here means a relationship that the parties to it have chosen, unlike, say, the relationship of parent to child, or brother to sister, which are natural relationships we do not choose. A covenant means a relationship with obligations, where each has made certain promises to the other and entered into commitments, in this case to be husband and wife, with all that that means.

And – here is the challenge and warning – it means a relationship with God as witness. God is not a third party to the covenant, but he is a witness. This means that, however few human witnesses may have been present, God is present when the promises are made. And he holds each of the parties responsible to keep their promises. The promises are made under his sanction. If the parties break them, they are answerable to him. We find this same idea in the context of another covenant in Genesis 31:50, where Laban says to his nephew Jacob as they make an agreement, 'Although no one else is with us, see, God is witness between you and me.' That is, don't even think of breaking this agreement, because God will punish you if you do. In the same way, God himself places the whole weight of his authority behind the marriage covenant (and that means all valid marriages, not just church marriages).

The reason God would not listen to the men's prayers in Malachi's day was that they had broken their marriage covenants and he was holding them to account. I doubt if they would have got a very friendly reception if they had replied that they 'had to divorce' because their feelings of love had now cooled or they had 'fallen out of love'. The heart of marriage is faithfulness to a promise, not going with the ebbs and flows of a romance.

God takes marriage very seriously. He does so because the marriage covenant is an echo of the covenant he makes by his own marriage with his people. In Ezekiel 16:8 God the Divine Husband says to 'Jerusalem' his bride, 'I made my vow to you and entered into a covenant with you ... and you became mine.' God is faithful to his covenant (as we shall see), and he calls us to be faithful in ours.

Marriage faithfulness excludes all rivals for life

> You shall not commit adultery.
> (Exodus 20:14)

Because marriage is a covenant to which God is witness, and a union which God joins, it follows that the heart of marriage is faithfulness that excludes rivals for life. 'You shall not commit adultery,' says the seventh commandment (Exodus 20:14). Adultery is consistently condemned as a very serious sin both in the Old Testament and in the New (e.g. Matthew 5:27–28). This marks out marriage as quite different from friendship.

For in friendship three are company, and four even better company. But in the sexual relationship anything more than two is adultery.

We need to understand why adultery is so serious. If you are engaged or happily married, you probably wonder if it is worth reading this section. After all, the thought of adultery appals you; you cannot imagine how you could ever be tempted towards it. But please don't skip this section. As always with right and wrong, the one who thinks he stands firmly needs to listen carefully and take care lest he fall (1 Corinthians 10:12). Even if you are not tempted to adultery just now, you may be quite sure that one day you will be. You will find yourself attracted to a neighbour, a friend, or a work colleague, and you will begin to give the attraction house room in your imagination, and then to wonder if all your principles need really be quite so rigid. Would it really be as bad as all that? It would, and here are six reasons why. I want you to see adultery for the dark and horrible thing it is.

Six reasons why adultery is very serious

It is turning away from a promise

> This is the way of an adulteress:
>   she eats and wipes her mouth
>   and says, 'I have done no wrong.'
> (Proverbs 30:20)

First, adultery is a turning away from a promise. The adulterer doesn't think it is a turning *away*. His mind is full of the lover *towards* whom he is turning, as he begins his affair with her (or she with him). He persuades himself, or she persuades herself, that it is in some way a good turning towards someone lovely and deserving. As the adulteress in Proverbs 30:20, she eats her forbidden fruit and, like a guest at a good dinner, 'wipes her mouth and says, "I have done no wrong."' But in its heart adultery is not a turning towards, but a turning away. Adulterers have made public pledges. They each promised before witnesses to be faithful to one particular woman or man until one of them died. And then they turned away from that promise, forsook that partner, and broke their word. And whether they realize it or not, God was one of the witnesses to their promises (Malachi 2:14).

It leads the adulterer from security to chaos

Adultery therefore leads to a divided life with torn loyalties. Once the promise is broken, the barrier is breached, the secure wall of marriage is torn down, all hell breaks loose. And an adulterer finds he or she has not after all exchanged one secure place (his marriage) for another secure place (the new home with the new partner).

Instead, adulterers find they have left the secure place and entered a world in which anything goes, in which faithfulness becomes a distant memory, and in which all too often a succession of further affairs and subsequent marriages ensue. I well remember a man having an affair and telling me that if he left his wife for this new woman, all would be well. He would settle down with her and make a new and better marriage. I warned him that he was introducing a destructive instability into his life, but he would not listen. Very sadly, the pattern since then has been of terrible instability, moving from one woman to another for longer or shorter periods.

And even when, by the grace of God, the adulterer does settle with a new woman and stay with her, even then he must live with a divided life, with memories of (and broken loyalties to) his first wife jostling for place in his affections alongside his present experience and new loyalty. To the adulterer, the grass seems so much greener the other side of the fence, but it isn't nearly as green as it looks.

It is secretive and dishonest

Adultery is inherently secretive. Because it is the breaking of a promise, no one wants to advertise it. No one wants to stand at the street corner and say, 'Look at me. You can't trust me. If you have any sense you won't believe a word I say.' And so adultery shrinks from publicity. As Job said, 'The eye of the adulterer . . . waits for the twilight, saying, "No eye will see me"; and he veils his face' (Job 24:15). Adultery prefers darkness. It may not succeed in remaining secret. But whereas news of a marriage is broadcast by joyful announcements and invitations, news of an adultery leaks out by rumour and under pressure. I remember a friend of mine whose wife had committed adultery telling me that in some ways it was the lying and secrecy that were the worst part of the whole wretched business.

It destroys the adulterer

It follows that adultery destroys the moral fabric of the adulterer. Like all secret sin, it eats away like some noxious chemical at the integrity of the one who commits it. The moment any of us drive a wedge between what we say we are publicly and what we actually are privately, we injure ourselves at the deepest possible level. I vividly remember listening to the agonized words of an old man who had been a Christian minister and now lay sick. He told me how he had been in Christian ministry, and how one act of adultery had ended his ministry and destroyed the moral fabric of his life. It was a very sad sight, a man so broken, and it was adultery that did it. I hope that as we looked at the promises of Jesus Christ together, and I prayed with him, there was a real experience of forgiveness and a measure of restoration. But even with the reality of forgiveness, the scars were still deep and painful.

It damages society

Adultery damages the fabric of society. Not only does it damage those directly involved, it also has knock-on effects on wider society. Each act of adultery is like a wrecker's ball taking a swing at the secure walls of the social fabric of society. It stirs up hatred and enmity. It encourages a culture which reckons marriage boundaries needn't really be quite so rigid.

Adulterers are not forced by society to become loners, or ostracized. Instead, they gather round them friends who will join in the same kind of behaviour and therefore make them feel good about the way they have behaved. Indeed, the friends may praise a male adulterer as 'having quite a way with the women'. Indeed he may have, but it is a very destructive way. So the psalmist laments to his hearers that 'you *keep company* with adulterers' (Psalm 50:18, my emphasis). And so, as adulterers' groups of friends grow, society as a whole begins to tolerate and then to approve this kind of behaviour (Romans 1:32).

We see this in practice. Maybe we know a man who committed adultery and is now living with somebody else. Perhaps he is a work colleague or a neighbour. What do we say? We are nervous about seeming to condemn him by expressing disapproval. And so we say, 'It was sad that his marriage broke down. But these things happen. And it's good that he seems happier now with his new woman.'

And then when I am tempted to adultery myself, the devil whispers in my ear, 'It would be sad if you were to leave your wife. A pity, yes, but not really much more than that. And just like that man you knew, you may find you settle down much more happily with a new woman. And society will get used to the change.' And so the safeguard of public disapproval of adultery gradually disintegrates.

It hurts children

Adultery harms children. Let's state it baldly like that. Children especially are hurt when a father or mother commits adultery. Because children are right in the thick of it, in the intimacy of the family home broken by cheating on promises, darkened by secrecy and lies, riven with conflict and hatreds. Adultery hurts children.

Flee adultery like the plague!

For all these reasons we need to understand that faithfulness is the heart of marriage. And faithfulness is enormously important. You may have ups and downs emotionally and relationally in marriage. But never break the exclusive marriage promise by getting into bed with anybody else, ever. And if you are reading this and have already committed adultery, be clear that the only way back is clear repentance, bringing it into the open before those affected, confessing it, painful as this will be. And then turn resolutely from it, breaking off all further contact with the person with whom you have committed adultery. In Jesus Christ forgiveness is available for all who will turn to him in repentance and faith. The Bible's teaching on sex and marriage is for moral failures, to offer forgiveness and to change us by the grace of God to live a new life.

Faithfulness in marriage is modelled on the faithfulness of God

It is a relief to turn back from the dark subject of adultery to the bright and wonderful subject of the faithfulness of God. We have seen that the reason that faithfulness lies at the heart of marriage is that faithfulness lies at the heart of God, and therefore at the heart of the universe. Those of us who are married are called to keep the covenant promises of marriage, because God keeps his covenant promises. He is the God who makes covenant promises and then keeps them without fail. And in particular, he makes covenant promises as the bridegroom or husband of his people, his bride. And he keeps the promises he has made. He keeps them in the teeth of opposition and in the face of the faithlessness of his bride. The story in the Bible of God's marriage is the story of one utterly faithful spouse married to one persistently faithless spouse. It is a story which shows at the same time the misery of adultery and the wonder of costly faithfulness. All who struggle with a difficult marriage need to enter into the pain and persistence of God himself as he struggles with his difficult marriage.

Perhaps the most vivid picture of this is given in Hosea. The prophet is told to marry a woman with a reputation, and probably a past that would keep most upright men a long way away.

> When the LORD first spoke through Hosea, the LORD said to Hosea, 'Go, take to yourself a wife of whoredom and have children of whoredom, for the land commits great whoredom by forsaking the LORD.'
> (Hosea 1:2)

Hosea does so, and it is the most excruciatingly painful dramatization in actual life of the pain God feels in his marriage to his people. But the extraordinary thing is that, in Hosea chapter 2, God makes breathtaking promises.

> [14]'Therefore, behold, I will allure her,
>   and bring her into the wilderness,
>   and speak tenderly to her.
> [15]And there I will give her her vineyards
>   and make the Valley of Achor a door of hope.
> And there she shall answer as in the days of her youth,
>   as at the time when she came out of the land of Egypt.
> (Hosea 2:14–15)

He promises to 'allure' her. This word 'allure' really means 'seduce' (as in Exodus 22:16), and is therefore a risky word to use! But in marriage there is a place for a good seduction, a drawing back and rekindling warmth in a relationship that has gone through tough times. This is what God does with his people.

He promises to his unfaithful wife, to 'bring her into the wilderness' (the place where she has good memories of trusting him), and 'speak tenderly to her'. To 'speak tenderly' means literally 'to speak to the heart', to touch the affections. This is what Boaz does to Ruth (Ruth 2:13) and what the Lord does to Jerusalem (Isaiah 40:2). This is covenant faithfulness in marriage: to keep the door of hope open, to welcome back, to forgive, even to 'seduce' back, and to do all in our power to build and rebuild our marriages.

This tenderness is very remarkable. His wife has hurt him abominably, deserting him and having affairs with rival after rival. And yet he takes her back with loving tenderness. Indeed, he will make 'the valley of Achor' (the place of trouble) into 'a door of hope'.

No marriage will survive, and certainly no damaged marriage can be repaired, without this forgiveness. The problem in marriage is often not that one spouse does wrong, but that the other will not forgive. One hurts the other or offends the other in some way. That is bad, and it damages marriage. But what if they repent, turn from the way they have behaved, and come to their spouse for forgiveness, hoping to be welcomed back, for the warmth gradually to return? What if now their repentance is thrown back in their face, they are not forgiven, and the chill remains unthawed?

Unforgiveness may even be more serious in its consequences than the original offence, because it stops reconciliation. It is much the same when forgiveness is supposedly offered (at least in word) and yet the offender is repeatedly reminded about what they have said or done. This makes it clear that the forgiveness they were offered is at best partial.

Faithfulness in marriage comes from the faithfulness of God

This brings us to a very important principle: not only is faithfulness in marriage modelled on the faithfulness of God, but faithfulness in marriage actually *comes* from the faithfulness of God. The point is this: it is not that God is faithful and I then do my best to be faithful like him. That would be a recipe for discouragement when I find I cannot do it in my own strength. Rather, it is that God is faithful and pours his grace and faithfulness into me, if I will come to him and trust him. This is a recipe for success, because the moral resources necessary for marriage are offered to me by the grace of God.

The difference is profound. If I think the Bible's teaching is basically moralizing, that it's just a case of being told how we ought to behave and then doing our best, I will never succeed. But once I realize the Bible's teaching is about grace, about God offering us the moral resources to build our marriages, then I can take courage.

> . . . bearing with one another and, if one has a complaint against another, forgiving each other; as the Lord has forgiven you, so you also must forgive.
> (Colossians 3:13)

This truth is put briefly by Paul in his letter to the Colossians, and taught more fully by Jesus himself in Matthew's Gospel. Writing to the Christians in Colossae, Paul told them that 'as the Lord has forgiven you, so you also must forgive' (Colossians 3:13). This is spoken to all Christians, not just to husbands and wives. Nevertheless it applies within a marriage. I am not told just to grit my teeth and forgive, for I cannot do that; I do not have it in myself. But I am told to forgive, *as the Lord Jesus has forgiven me*. His forgiveness of me is like a river that flows into my life and then on out of my life, as I forgive others. Jesus teaches this same truth in Matthew 18:21–35.

[21]Then Peter came up and said to him, 'Lord, how often will my brother sin against me, and I forgive him? As many as seven times?' [22]Jesus said to him, 'I do not say to you seven times, but seventy times seven.

[23]'Therefore the kingdom of heaven may be compared to a king who wished to settle accounts with his servants ...

[35]'So also my heavenly Father will do to every one of you, if you do not forgive your brother from your heart.'
(Matthew 18:21–23, 35)

Matthew 18, like Colossians 3, is about how Christians ought to behave with one another. Simon Peter (so often it was Peter!) asks the question in verse 21: 'Lord, how often will my brother sin against me and I forgive him?' The implication is that this fellow Christian has repented and asked forgiveness (cf. Luke 17:3–4). So he hurts me, he does something against me, and then he turns from it and he asks my forgiveness, and I forgive him.

And then he does it again, and again, and again! This is the problem: how to live with ongoing troubles in a relationship?

Jesus' answer is profound. He tells the famous story of the two servants in a grand household. One owes the master an astronomical debt, something more than all the money in circulation at the time, trillions of pounds. The master forgives him and sets him free. This servant then meets a fellow-servant who owes him a few months' salary. Not a trivial debt at all, a significant amount, although a million or so times smaller than the debt he had just been forgiven. He won't forgive, but imprisons his fellow-servant until he pays. The master is outraged and the unforgiving servant is severely punished.

The point of the story is not to say to us, 'You really must forgive one another; forgiveness is very, very important.' That is true, but would not actually help. When, especially in a marriage, a hurt is done, it is very hard to forgive. And just being told to forgive doesn't work. No, the point of the story is that you and I need to understand the astronomical debt we have been forgiven if we are disciples of Christ. And once we begin to grasp this truth, the gates of our hearts are opened so that we can forgive even very serious debts owed to us. God works in us to enable us to forgive.

This truth means that the best possible basis on which to build marriage is real Christian faith. Marriage is not easy for any couple. Conflict is hard to resolve and hurts are hard to forgive. If we are to do the whole thing with only our own moral resources, it will be very hard and may prove impossible.

But once we really know the forgiveness that Jesus Christ offers, there is in our hearts a new dynamic. Grace pours into our hearts, and that same grace can pour out from our hearts to our husbands and wives to forgive, to heal, to reconcile, to follow hurts with welcome, and conflict with tenderness.

What you and I need most of all is to know the steadfast faithful love of the God who has never broken a promise yet. He kept every promise he has ever made when he sent his Son Jesus Christ to die in our place. He is utterly faithful and trustworthy. If we will turn afresh to him and come to him in trusting obedience, we can rest our security in his mercy. And on that basis, building on that security, we will be well placed to show faithfulness in marriage, to offer forgiveness when hurt, and to welcome back with tenderness even when things are at their most painful. In a society of sexual chaos, what we need above all is not to be lectured with stern moralizing but to open our hearts to the steadfast love of the faithful Lover God.

For study or discussion

1. a. What does 'one flesh' union mean?

b. Who is joined in 'one flesh' union?

c. Who joins them?

2. In what ways do human beings break marriages, their own and other people's? Think practically about how marriages go wrong, and whose fault it is.

3. What does it mean to say that marriage is a covenant?

4. What does God mean by saying he is witness to the covenant?

5. Why is adultery so serious?

6. What are the danger points in your marriage, when you may begin to be tempted to adultery?
   a. Is pornography available to you, on the internet, on television, in magazines? How can you avoid it and keep your sexual desires entirely focused on your wife or husband?

   b. Do you travel on business? If so, what safeguards do you need to put in place to protect your marriage?

c. Are there situations at work where you need to draw boundaries in how you relate to colleagues of the opposite sex?

d. What are the particular stresses of your marriage that can make it seem as if the grass is greener elsewhere? How can you anticipate these times and be prepared for them? Think about times like childbirth, bereavement, times of anticlimax after a big work commitment, times when you want to relax and you are away from home.

7. a. What does it mean to say that God is faithful?

b. How does this show us how to behave in our marriages?

8. a. How does conflict arise in our marriages?

b. How do you and your husband or wife set about resolving conflict?

c. In what situations do you find it hard to forgive?

d. How does the gospel of Jesus Christ contain the key to our forgiveness in marriage? And how can you remind yourselves of this gospel truth together?

Conclusion: The greatest invitation

Let us rejoice and exult
    and give him the glory,
for the marriage of the Lamb has come,
    and his Bride has made herself ready.
(Revelation 19:7)

²And I saw the holy city, new Jerusalem, coming down out of heaven from God, prepared as a bride adorned for her husband. ³And I heard a loud voice from the throne saying, 'Behold, the dwelling place of God is with man. He will dwell with them, and they will be his people, and God himself will be with them as their God. ⁴He will wipe away every tear from their eyes, and death shall be no more, neither shall there be mourning nor crying nor pain any more, for the former things have passed away.'
   . . . ⁹'Come, I will show you the Bride, the wife of the Lamb.'
(Revelation 21:2–4, 9)

Every human being can be married in the end, if they want to be. That applies to those who have never married and may never marry in this life. It applies to those divorced, whether or not it was mainly or even entirely their fault. It is true for widows. Whatever sexual desires and longings you have, whatever your history of experience or inexperience, delights or frustrations, right behaviour or misbehaviour, you can know all your longings fulfilled in the end, if you want that. Every human being is invited to be married in the end, and not only to be married, but to be blissfully married in the marriage to beat all marriages. The only question is whether or not we will accept this invitation.

The Bible tells many stories of human marriages, both good and bad, from Adam and Eve through Abraham and Sarah, David and Bathsheba, and countless others. All of them, one way or another, are stories of dysfunctional people in spoiled relationships.

But above these stories the Bible tells a bigger story, the story of a marriage which includes within itself the whole history and future of the human race. It is the story of God the Lover, the Bridegroom, the Husband, and his people his Beloved, his Bride, and in the end his Wife. It is the story that John the Baptist had in mind when he spoke of Jesus as the 'Bridegroom' (John 3:25–30), and the story that Jesus himself accepted when he spoke of himself as the 'Bridegroom' (e.g. Matthew 9:14–15). It is the story Paul referred to when he spoke of the church in Corinth being 'engaged' to Jesus Christ like a pure virgin (2 Corinthians 11:2).

It is the story that John speaks of in the visionary imagery of Revelation 19 and 21. The metaphors are mixed and the language is vivid and suggestive; we cannot read it literally and it would not be possible to make a film of this imagery. At the climax of human history John hears the announcement, 'The marriage of the Lamb has come, and his Bride has made herself ready' (Revelation 19:7). The Lamb, the Lord Jesus Christ himself, is to be married at last. His Bride is his people, every believer of all time, corporately to be joined to him forever in a union of unmixed delight and intimacy. This is a time of joy and amazement. And then, in Revelation 21, John sees the heavenly Jerusalem, that is, the whole new heavens and new earth, the restored and redeemed created order, coming down out of heaven as a city, but not only a city, also a bride, 'prepared as a bride adorned for her husband'. For this renewed and restored creation is 'the bride, the wife of the Lamb' (Revelation 21:2, 9). All of the people of God in the new heavens and new earth are the bride of Jesus Christ. That is to say, he loves them passionately, and they love him with an answering love.

And in that new age their love will be consummated with an intimacy and enduring delight that the best human marriage can only begin faintly to echo. To put it bluntly, the most climactic and rapturous delight ever experienced in sexual intimacy by a married couple in the history of the human race cannot hold a candle to the delight of that union.

This is an amazing and beautiful prospect: a time when all the deepest yearnings and longings of the human heart will be fulfilled. And it is open to all who will come in repentance and faith to Jesus Christ in this age. The invitation is open.

Every time an unmarried person feels frustrated or depressed by their circumstances and unfulfilled desires, this is a pointer to the age to come. Jesus Christ says to them, 'Set your sights on your wedding day, which is also my wedding day. You think you are "on the shelf"? Not at all, for I love you passionately.'

Every time a married person struggles with conflict or pain in marriage it is a signpost to the age to come. Jesus Christ says to them, 'Lift your eyes above the frustrations and pain and look up to that wedding day, when I will take all my people in my arms forever.'

Every time a man or woman feels the pain of the scars of past mistakes and hurts, Jesus says to them, 'Look up to that wedding day. Because in that wedding you will wear spotless pure clothes, and the only scars in that wedding will be the scars I bore for you, the scars on my feet, in my hands and my side. Because I bore those scars, there will be none on you.'

On that day all the sex within marriage that has been used in the service of God in this age will be taken up into an eternity of sexual fulfilment which will fill the age to come with delight, security and wonder to beat all marriages. May God help us to be there to enjoy it.

For study or discussion

1. Whatever your circumstances, married or single, happy or unhappy, fulfilled or frustrated, will you now bring it all to the God who loves you, and accept his invitation to become a part of the Bride of Jesus Christ?

2. If you are a Christian, will you meditate on the marriage of the Lamb and take to that marriage all your pains, hurts, frustrations and struggles in the areas of sex and marriage?

3. Finally, will you pray for the grace of God to accept your current circumstances as his gift to you, and to learn contentment within them?

Further reading

In 2003 I wrote *Marriage: Sex in the Service of God* (IVP). This is a thorough biblical and theological study intended for church ministers, theological students and those who run marriage preparation or marriage enrichment courses. You will find most of the references, sources of quotations, detailed arguments, and more, in this longer study, which is referred to below as *Marriage*. I have linked the chapters in this book to the relevant pages in *Marriage*.

General

John and Ann Benton, *Don't They Make a Lovely Couple?* (Christian Focus Publications, 2005) is a short, readable and practical introduction to marriage.

Michael and Myrtle Baughen, *Your Marriage* (Hodder & Stoughton, 1994) is an attractively produced and illustrated practical guide for engaged couples.

Tony Payne and Phillip D. Jensen, *Pure Sex* (Matthias Media, 1997) is a lucid critique of the sexual revolution of the 1960s, and shows how much better is the Christian alternative.

Geoffrey W. Bromiley, *God and Marriage* (Wipf and Stock, 2003) is a concise and perceptive theological study of marriage.

Andreas Köstenberger, *God, Marriage, and Family: Rebuilding the Biblical Foundation* (Crossway Books, 2004) is a comprehensive biblical study of a very wide range of questions related to marriage and family.

Introduction: God at the centre

Marriage, pp. 15, 16 on God and sex; pp. 39–45 on the breakdown of relationships; pp. 103–106 on the purpose of God.

Chapter 1: A word about baggage and grace

Marriage, pp. 24–33 on prejudice and grace.

Chapter 2: Sex in the service of God

Marriage, pp. 106–111 on the three 'goods' of marriage; and pp. 112–132 on 'sex in the service of God'.

Chapter 3: What is the point of having children?

Marriage, pp. 38, 39 on trends in society; and pp. 157–184 on children in the service of God.

Chapter 4: What is the point of sex and intimacy?

Marriage, pp. 45–53 on changing attitudes to sex in society; pp. 133–156 on making sex an idol; and pp. 185–199 on how sex and intimacy serve God.

For practical help on sex and intimacy, see Trevor Stammers, *The Family Guide to Sex and Intimacy* (Hodder & Stoughton, 1994), or Ed and Gaye Wheat, *Intended for Pleasure: Sex Technique and Sexual Fulfilment in Christian Marriage*, 3rd edn (Scripture Union, 2000).

Chapter 5: God's pattern for the marriage relationship?

Marriage, pp. 272–339 on God's pattern for marriage.
These questions of headship and submission are the subject of much debate. For a useful volume by various authors who generally share my understanding, see Wayne Grudem (ed.), *Biblical Foundations for Manhood and Womanhood* (Crossway Books, 2002).

Chapter 6: What is the point of the marriage institution?

Marriage, pp. 34–38 on social patterns of cohabitation; pp. 53–55 on attitudes to marriage as a process rather than an institution; pp. 55–59 on church attitudes to cohabitation and sex outside marriage; pp. 63–82 on marriage as part of the created order; pp. 204–207 on how the institution of marriage serves God; pp. 211–245 on the definition of marriage and consent; and pp. 246–255 on one man and one woman.
Patricia Morgan, *Marriage-Lite: The Rise of Cohabitation and its Consequences* (London: Institute for the Study of Civil Society, 2000) gives a clear social critique of cohabitation.
Robert A. J. Gagnon, *The Bible and Homosexual Practice: Texts and Hermeneutics* (Abingdon Press, 2002) is the definitive work showing that homosexual practice is defined as sinful in the Bible.

Thomas E. Schmidt, *Straight and Narrow? Compassion and Clarity in the Homosexuality Debate* (IVP, 1995) covers the main biblical material clearly, but also has very helpful medical and pastoral material.

Chapter 7: Is it better to stay single?

Al Hsu, *The Single Issue* (IVP, 1997, with an appendix by John Stott) covers the practical and pastoral issues of singleness much more deeply than I have been able to do.

Chapter 8: What is the heart of marriage?

Marriage, pp. 340–367 on faithfulness.
Elisabeth Elliot, *Passion and Purity: Learning to Bring your Love Life under Christ's Control*, 2nd edn (Revell, 2002) is something of a classic devotional book.

Conclusion: The greatest invitation

Marriage, pp. 87–89 on the fulfilment of marriage in the new creation.

Suggestions for uses of the study questions

Including marriage preparation and marriage refreshment

There are probably too many questions at the ends of the chapters for most people to feel they want to work through them all. They are there as a resource. Here are some suggestions as to how you might use them.

Individual use

Whether you are married or not, you may wish to use the book for a programme of private study about marriage. If you do this, it will be important to allow yourself time not only to think about the questions but also to respond quietly in prayer.

Marriage preparation

An engaged couple can use it together in marriage preparation, with or without a church leader to help them. I suggest you read a chapter at a time and jot down your answers to the questions separately, on your own, before coming together to talk about what you have written and to discuss how you might respond.

Marriage refreshment

A married couple can also use it to provide an informal marriage refresher. Again, I suggest reading a chapter at a time and writing down your responses individually before coming together to talk it over and agree how you will respond.

Church course

A church may find it helpful to use the book as the basis for a course of either marriage preparation or marriage refreshment for couples. In this case I strongly suggest the leaders do background study from *Marriage: Sex in the Service of God* as part of their preparation. You will probably wish to guide the members of the course as to which questions to tackle together and which to ponder privately. You may wish to supplement the questions with some of your own, suited to your own church context and needs.

discover more great Christian books
at www.ivpbooks.com

Full details of all the books from Inter-Varsity Press – including
reader reviews, author information, videos and free downloads –
are available on our website at **www.ivpbooks.com**.

IVP publishes a wide range of books on various subjects including:

Biography

Christian Living

Bible Studies

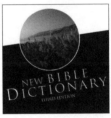

Reference

Commentaries

Theology

On the website you can also sign up for regular email newsletters,
tell others what you think about books you have read by posting
reviews, and locate your nearest Christian bookshop using the
Find a Store feature.

IVP publishes Christian books that are **true to the Bible**
and that **communicate the gospel, develop discipleship**
and **strengthen the church** for its mission in the world.